LINES to the HORIZON

LINES to the HORIZON

HORIZON

Australian Surf Writing

Foreword by
Jock Serong

FREMANTLE PRESS

Contents

Foreword – Jock Serong

When I started submitting work to surfing magazines, long before I dreamed of writing fiction, I tried to follow an identifiable set of footprints. It was a small enough scene at that stage that you could meet the entirety of it during happy hour at the Torquay pub on Easter Saturday. Especially if you were running a tab.

The Australian writers I could find back then were Derek Hynd, Andrew Kidman, Phil Jarratt and Nick Carroll. Kidman infused his writing with wisdom from other realms: his interests in music, filmmaking and design. Hynd was an outlier, raging and clawing at the Establishment. Jarratt and Carroll operated as prolific, well-connected sports journos with, in Jarratt's case, an instinct for business writing.

There was the odd hybrid of a different sort, like Michael Gordon, the nationally respected journalist who was equally at home writing about the archaeology of the Dreamtime, federal politics or the history of Bells Beach. His early death was a loss to both journalism and surfing.

Then came a generation of highly entertaining writer/editors with a side-hustle in long-form biography—Sean Doherty, Tim Baker and Derek Reilly. It was a smart ruse—easiest Christmas present in the world, Mum: the Fanning book. This generation of writers—and by this stage, I too—was backed by great editors like Keith Curtain, Vaughan Blakey and Luke Kennedy: people who haven't had mega-budgets to throw at projects, but who burn with a phosphorescent passion for surfing, its protagonists and scribes.

The names I've reeled off are each exceptional craftsmen. But they're exclusively male, and their realm is non-fiction. That's partially a reflection of my experience, and partially me bumping at the disappointing limits of the culture: there has yet to be a female editor of a major surf media outlet in this country. Favel Parrett surfs and writes award-winning fiction (and therefore, by conjunction, is a surf-writer); Rebecca Olive is doing innovative academic work about surfing, gender and society; and Sally Breen straddles the worlds of academic writing, fiction and commentary. Madelaine Dickie wrote *Troppo*, rich with Indonesian surfing references, before I'd dreamed of *On the Java Ridge*. But only *Surfing World*'s Lauren Hill and *Tracks*' Emily Brugman come to mind as regular female surfing correspondents in Australia. It's not enough. The women who appear in this book are carriers of a vital flame.

This is not to say that women are under-represented in our surfing history: Isabel Letham was as much a part of the birth of Australian surfing at Freshwater as the Duke himself. It is to say that the contribution of our women needs to be given a voice.

From the early, underpaid pioneers like Pam Burridge, Jodie Cooper and Pauline Menczer, through to the era of elite athletes like Layne Beachley, Stephanie Gilmore and Tyler Wright, our female surfers have dominated the world. All around our coast now, girls are growing up in the expectation that the line-up is theirs, as much as it is the blokes'. Middle-aged women who endured a longstanding culture of machismo and territorial aggression in the water are now seeing their perseverance rewarded. Boorishness remains, sadly, but I know my daughters can see role models, and they'll become examples themselves, with time.

In 2016, I embarked on a little writing exercise. I'd rarely, if ever, read fiction about surfing that avoided cliché and found an essence that surfers and non-surfers could agree upon. The stand-out exceptions, to me, were Malcolm Knox's *The Life* (a thinly veiled portrait of the Peterson family) and Tim Winton's coming-of-age novel *Breath* (Mark Smith's Winter trilogy, with its riff on post-apocalyptic empty line-ups, was yet to come). *Breath* conveyed the elemental terror of a deep, dark hold-down to people who had never experienced one. After my mum read the book she said something like 'Now I understand what you boys were on about ...' As far as I know, she wasn't referring to autoerotic asphyxiation.

The exercise I set myself was to try writing a little passage of surfing fiction. I wrote about a girl on a wave in the tropics, and the handful of paragraphs grafted itself mysteriously onto a rant I was writing about our treatment of refugees. The result was a novel called *On the Java Ridge* and, to my ongoing delight, the brief passage about the girl surfing survived countless rounds of edits and made the final pages.

The point of the story, I think, is that writing about surfing is harder than it looks. Surfing by its very nature is ephemeral: whatever is written upon a wave is instantly erased. Nobody can agree whether this is a sport, or a culture, a sensual entwining with nature itself, a dance, or a form of meditation ... or none of these. Emily Brugman writes of the sea's pitiless indifference: the Wintonian notion that 'I love the sea, but it does not love me'. Wandering through Mexico, Madelaine Dickie sees the ocean as refuge, and the land as a malevolent realm. Yet the other side of the very same ocean can offer Sally Breen a fecund source of urban culture, rich enough to feed a lifetime of watching people and writing about them.

So who *are* the surfers? Whose language do you use? The contradictions will never be resolved. A lifetime of doing it leaves you with just as many unanswered questions as the day you started.

In these pages, three men join Breen, Brugman and Dickie. Jake Sandtner has conjured a claustrophobic intimacy with the racing thoughts inside Taj Burrow's head. For Sam Carmody, writing about surfing is an exploration of one's own soul, a search for slow healing. And Mark Smith studies the surfing lives of others with a clear-eyed detachment that finds still more motives for doing what we do: for partaking in a reverse penguin-parade that defies all definition but makes perfect sense.

The six pieces show it is the immersion and the articulation that is important, not the perfection. The opening of a wave pool in Melbourne has pushed this ambiguity into the foreground. My friends go regularly: I have no desire to join them. All the perfect waves you could ever want, customised, on demand, and the idea leaves me flat. Despite calling myself a writer, I have neither the nouns and verbs, nor the sequence of thoughts, to describe why that is. Perhaps I'm just a grump. Perhaps it's imperfection that we writers chase.

Writing about surfing is more important for Australians than it ever was. Such is surfing's dominance in our self-image that to understand the nation it is necessary to interrogate the paddlers of Snapper, Bondi, Shipsterns, Gnaraloo and the countless, nameless sandbank peaks in between. Scientists have recently come to a new understanding of cool temperate reefs in Australia—that all of them are linked by an identifiable common biology into one vast biomass: the Great Southern Reef, stretching from Kalbarri to the Tweed. The other thing that links them is the surfers floating above. We are part of this.

Surfers live the change of days, of seasons, of the climate itself, every time they paddle out. Standing in the carpark, peering at lines in the half-dark, we are collecting data. I would venture to say there is no greater store of data about coastal conditions, accumulating in real time, every single day, around sixty thousand kilometres of coastline, than that which is collected in all our salty heads. We grunt under our beanies, but we *notice things*. When we can harness that decentralised matrix of observation, we will understand more acutely our disproportionate and damaging role in deep time.

So we need a literary culture around our surfing. What we see individually dies with us unless we share it as a body of knowledge. The revolutionary spirit in which Australians have led the world in designing equipment, in exploring coasts, in trying new approaches, needs now to aggregate into a published canon. We need to elevate the discussion, and not feel cynical about that. We need to bring in the voices that haven't been heard yet, and to use surfing discussions to foster other, harder discussions: about activism, mental health, environmental decline, Indigeneity, gender, getting old ... about the very nature of work and play.

We need to dare to throw out the old vocabularies. We have been ably led by the first generations of surf writers in Australia, and, as this collection demonstrates, our horizons are unlimited.

Following the Birds
Madelaine Dickie

Guerrero

1.

One morning in 2014, some surfers were driving out to The Ranch—a once-secret wave on Mexico's Guerrero coast. They passed rain-eaten concrete and a stinking mango factory. They wondered what the surf would be like. On a good day, the wave ran for nearly a kilometre, with barrel sections and a workable, whackable wall. As they approached a bridge, the driver slowed.

Up ahead, a row of dead bodies dangled by their necks.

I hear this story in my first week in Mexico and suspect I should have done better research before leaving. Sure, I'd read about the cartel bosses, fabled for feeding human hearts to their teenage employees; and the boiled bones in the country's north, evidence of ritual cannibalism among the Xiximes; and I'd read about the cuisine, with its dizzyingly difficult names, like *chilaquiles*, and *chapulines*, and *mole* and *mezcal*. But I hadn't bothered to check the Australian Government's advice for Guerrero—hadn't 'reconsidered my need to travel'. And even if I had, the promise of exotic waves generally trumps risk. I think surf travel is a bit like following the birds.

2.

My last Sunday at home on Western Australia's Ningaloo Reef brings conditions locally described as 'glamour'. The wind has finally quit punishing the desert and the water off the back of the reef has turned a thrilling blue—a shade promising pelagic fish. My husband Tom and I launch the tinny at our favourite reef pass.

We leave behind the rasping throats of gullies several months dry. We leave behind the land that once cradled the most ancient beaded necklace in the world. It's not long before we're following gannets and white terns and shearwaters. The birds' smoke-quick shadows skate the water, draw us toward the horizon. In our wake, the lines from our trolling rods dip and sway.

Then a hit! The waspish scream of the reel! The rod doubles and Tom shouts, 'Fuck, we're on! It's massive! Maybe we've foul-hooked a shark? A manta? A dolphin?'

The tinny's listing from side to side. The curses are coming thick and quick and salty. Suddenly a marlin, lit up with colours vivid as poison, streaks across the sky.

Over the next forty minutes, as Tom works the fish toward the boat to unhook it, I think about the birds—how they're a dangerous addiction. When I travel for waves, I carry the birds with me, in my brain, in my breast; they toss restless, tow me from the solid footing of land into the unknown, toward the promise of the next hook-up; perhaps a wave barrelling pink under prickly pear at dawn, or an exhibition in which violence is given form through embroidery, or a shady plaza in the mountains where an old man sees me crying and offers his hand for a dance.

My last weekend on the Ningaloo Coast is sublime. But once those wings start beating, they're impossible to ignore.

3.

I'm anxious about touching down in Mexico City alone, after four flights and over twenty-four hours without sleep. I've read of people robbed at the moneychangers inside Benito Juárez's international arrivals terminal; I've been warned of charlatans in fake taxis ready to skim the pesos from my purse, or to kidnap me. Then there are the stories of the ghost. A little girl, in Victorian-era clothing, is said to haunt the empty corridors and planes.

I think I'm more frightened of the taxi drivers, though a kidnapping might prove a challenge with my surfboards. I'm travelling with a 5'6" twin fin for soft, burgery waves, and a 6'3" step-up that I shaped myself with the help of my friend Dave.[1] I'd originally designed the step-up for windy winter mornings

15

at home, but I'm hoping it will also be good for Oaxaca's throaty right-hand point breaks. My rucksack's straining at the seams with fifteen books, ink pencils, an eighth of a new manuscript, three pairs of swimmers and a Spanish dictionary.

Eager to avoid hassle, I spend my first night in Mexico at the airport hotel and the following morning, I board a flight to Zihuatanejo, on Guerrero's steamy, rain-whipped coast. Guerrero is one of Mexico's poorest states. It's where forty-three young men went missing in 2014. The men were trainee teachers and had commandeered buses in the city of Iguala ahead of an annual pilgrimage to Mexico City to commemorate the Tlatelolco massacre. Hundreds of people were killed in the massacre, most of them university or high school–aged students.

In the case of Guerrero's missing forty-three, the 'missing' is a euphemism for 'murdered'. The young students never made it to Mexico City. Their buses became the target of five separate armed attacks. Two students were found dead. Walls and benches were found spattered with blood. But no-one found the forty-three young men.

Blame was initially cast on Guerreros Unidos, a local cartel alleged to have mistaken the students for members of a rival gang. The cartel was accused of burning the bodies in a rubbish tip and then disposing of the remains in a nearby river.[2] But forensic reports from the tip showed no signs of remains. In 2018, Mexican journalist Anabel Hernández released a meticulous investigation into the disappearance, titled *A Massacre in Mexico*.[3] She writes that the case smelled so rotten, the closer you got to it, the harder it was to breathe. Despite the proximity of security bases held by municipal, state and federal police, nothing was done to stop the attacks, or to prevent the disappearance of the students. In her book, Hernández exposes a web of complicity and suggests the blame falls with former president Peña Nieto's government. She writes, 'In the midst of Mexico's polarization and loneliness, people have forgotten that the pain caused by injustice against another should also be our own pain.'

Nos faltan 43.

In the months to come, I'll see this slogan on placards, online, and in the graphic design studios of Oaxaca City. *Nos faltan 43.*

We're missing 43.

4.

I reach the coastal village of Troncones in the late afternoon. Organ pipe cacti throw cool shadows across the road. Between villas of terracotta and cream, I catch glimpses of the surf. It's glassy. In my imagination, I'm out there, feeling the water like hot silk on my arms, feeling the germs from the plane slough from my skin.

The taxi driver is a young woman who is patient with my poor verb conjugations. She tells me most of the land here is in foreign hands. Locals can't afford to buy property. Instead, they're trucked in to work as gardeners, housekeepers and cooks. I'm staying in an Airbnb that's perhaps an exception to the rule. It's owned by a Mexican surfer, Winter, a fellow goofy-footer who studied in Santa Cruz. He rents out an open-air wooden cabin, way up in the trees. It's screened from the road by flowering vines and bamboo. There's a percolator, a hammock, a writing desk and wine glasses.

I can hear the sea.

I wax up, dance around some barbed wire, then cross an empty block to the beach.

The surf looks shifty, punchy, fun. Pelicans pass by in single file, gliding in gentle S-curves just above the water. There's a blood-red burley of storm clouds around the setting sun. A story comes back to me, the one about the American surfer attacked here by a shark a few months ago.

Maybe that's why there's no-one else out.

I'm not usually frightened by stories. At least, that's what I tell myself, as I paddle into the fading light.

5.

Jet lag jostles me from under the mozzie net at two am. I pack a percolator with coffee and set up with my writing journal at the desk. The pages stir. The truth is, I'm often frightened by stories, particularly when the stories harden into news. I was horrified to hear about the two Australian surfers murdered in Mexico in 2015.[4] Dean Lucas and Adam Coleman were both my age, thirty-three. They were travelling by van from the Baja California Peninsula across to mainland Mexico by car ferry. Coleman was racing to Guadalajara to meet his girlfriend. Honouring the meeting time was going to involve driving all night. Mexico's highways are dangerous at night.

The men were shot by bandits.

The van they were travelling in was torched.

Why do we do it, wander the most hazardous coasts of the world in search of waves? For me, I love the rhythm of a surf trip: the intense physicality of surfing for six hours a day, eating twice a day, walking to and from the beach, feeling sunburnt, feeling bruisingly sore deep under the shoulder blades. I love having the time to refine my style. Surfing's no longer something I do thoughtlessly, or mindlessly. I'm hungry. I have goals. Along these coasts, there's the thrill in language, too. I love threading words together in a second language, love the way the most banal of transactions, like buying surf wax or fixing a blown motorbike tyre, carry an extra linguistic challenge.

On this trip, when Tom gets in for the final manic month of the three that I'm here, I want to work on my backhand tube riding. I've only ever been barrelled for a moment, not long enough to see the world properly framed by a half-moon of water.

I check my phone. It's now two forty in the morning, a nowhere hour, a nightmare hour. From somewhere close comes a low roll of thunder.

I think again of Lucas and Coleman. Of the media reports on cartel-related violence and the Netflix export *Narcos*. I wonder if things here in Mexico are really as dangerous as the foreign press would have us believe. And if they are as bad, how are contemporary Mexican artists and writers coming to terms with the poison of violence in their communities, and in their country?

The first drops of rain begin to peck at the timber roof. I refill my coffee. I know these questions, now articulated, will keep nudging me, will demand my attention in the days and months to come.

6.

Playa La Saladita, a left-hander popular with longboarders, is about half an hour from Troncones. For three consecutive years it has been the location of the Mexi Log Fest, a competition that draws surfers from all over the world. Now, one of the musclier swells of winter is set to arrive, and I'm banking on it being too big for the beginners and some of the less experienced longboarders. Sure enough, once the sets start rolling in at the four-foot mark, there's only a handful of us vying for position out the back. The walls of the waves offer spacious, smooth canvases, perfect for the swoop and glide of my new twinny. I'm working on opening up my whole body as I swing through turns, I'm spreading my arms like wings, delighted with the speed, the rhythm and the different lines the board draws.

On the biggest afternoon of the swell, I get talking between sets to an Aussie chick from Byron drifting solo through Mexico. She asks where else I've been, and I tell her Troncones. She asks if I heard about the American woman.

'Nah, nothing. What woman?'

Unlike Lucas and Coleman, the American woman was driving in broad daylight. It was nine thirty in the morning. She'd just finished a yoga class in Troncones and was taking the highway back to Playa La Saladita when a car slammed on its brakes in front of her. Four men jumped out with guns and levelled them at her windscreen. She hit the accelerator and swung a hard U-turn, almost knocking down one of the men. Then she drove until they disappeared from the rear-view mirror, until her breathing slowed and her hands stopped shaking.

This was a month or so ago.

I wonder what I would do, if I were in her shoes. Climb out, hand over the keys, start walking?

The Aussie chick tells me the highway has a reputation as a popular dumping ground for dead bodies. I imagine a kettle of black, leather-faced vultures. I suspect Guerrero is a place where following the birds doesn't always mean finding fish.

7.

The last time I saw vultures, albeit a different type, was a little under a year ago in Senegal. I was doing research for a novel about a French madame running a black magic racket. She was smuggling the penises of albinos into neighbouring Mali to be used in potions. The story was to be rapid and wicked, a nod to Denis Johnson's *The Laughing Monsters*, and peopled with musicians, expats, Chinese investors, and 'sex tourists'—retired European women with drop-dead gorgeous young Senegalese men. The albinos-for-black-magic tale is not quite as absurd as it might sound. Many years ago, when I was in Mozambique, I got yarning with a waiter whose albino brother had been dismembered for magic. In another instance, from 2018, I'd learned about a five-year-old albino girl who was ritually killed and beheaded in the Malian town of Fana.

Obviously, a lot of work needed to be done to set up a respectful framework for the story, a lot of thinking. But unfortunately, as tends to be the case when I'm drifting the coasts of the world, I ended up doing more surfing than thinking, and almost no writing at all.

One of the surf spots high on my list to visit in Senegal was N'Gor Island, famous for a right-hand wave featured in the 1966 surf classic *The Endless Summer*. I waited for a boat across the channel in the shadows of half-finished skyscrapers and wheeling black vultures. The air was dark with a blustering dust from the Sahara, and the beach doubled as a rubbish tip and sewer. Once I'd crossed the channel, settled in to a basic Airbnb, and had a few surfs on N'Gor Right, I ventured to the left-hand wave at the other end of the island. It looked good: super long, no-one surfing, the water crystal clear. I paddled out. My leg-rope dragged on my ankle, weighed down by long ribbons of rubbish. A nappy floated past. I got out the back and sat up on my board. Millions of bits of plastic, the size of baby jellyfish, drifted around my legs.

It's a different story here in Mexico. The ocean seems healthy, teeming with schools of pelagic fish. The debris on the beaches is organic. The water is clean.

Isn't that shameful? I think. Isn't that sad?

When plastic-free water comes as a surprise, a treat, the exception and not the rule.

8.

My old friend Bina picks me up from Playa La Saladita for a mission to The Ranch. Bina's a smart, beer-loving, hard-charging Bavarian, who lives with her Mexican boyfriend in Zihuatanejo. She's quadrilingual, works as a translator, is bewitched by Guerrero and its waves, and is more saddened than fearful of the violence in her adopted country. Her preferred mode of transport is a VW bug that rattles with empty Corona bottles and wouldn't be roadworthy in most other parts of the world. Every time we slow for a *tope* or *reductor*— those ubiquitous Mexican speed bumps—the car conks out and she has to kick it in the guts to get it going again.

Years ago, we surfed together under a full moon at Pavones in Costa Rica. I caught a bomb: I remember taking off purely by feel and then just standing there, blindly, letting my fingers skim moon shadow. I rode it all the way to the fishermen's shacks at the end of the beach, where I was slammed among rolling tree logs and a cascade of cobblestones. When I got to my feet, my knees were covered in blood, and I was shaking with so much adrenaline I could barely walk.

We reminisce on that night as we head down a rat maze of unmarked dirt tracks toward The Ranch. This morning, there are no bodies swinging dead from any of the bridges, no roadblocks or men with guns.

As we near the surf, Bina tells me about another wave nearby, a big, nacho-chip left–right peak in front of a gated community called Rancho Palo Alto. You need to know the combination of the lock to get in, or someone who's got a house there. Or you need to buy land. The community's listed on International Surf Properties and the sales pitch boasts exclusivity and a way to escape reality through '… ownership and easy access to amazing surf…' It also champions socially responsible development through '… putting the locals to work…'[5]

'Putting the locals to work' is an unfortunate choice of words but the other thing that doesn't sit well with me is the idea of 'ownership' of a surf spot. At home, I don't need to be wealthy or privileged to access a wave. I don't need a key, permission, or to pay someone to go for a surf.

In any case, the VW bumps its way down a sandy track without bogging and we get a look at the once-secret left-hander that is The Ranch. Long, groomed lines peel down a kilometre-long reef. It's busy; maybe thirty people. And it's pumping. If I'd actually paused to watch a proper set, I would have been anxious on the paddle out and perhaps would have opted for my bigger board. But as usual, I'm in a rush, with no time for stretching, barely time for sunscreen, too busy imagining my first, swooping turn.

Six hours in the surf, six margaritas and six tacos later, I'm not feeling very well. That night, all night, I'm violently crook at half-hour intervals. The next morning's a travel day and I'm worried I'll shit myself either in the taxi, at the airport or on the plane. It wouldn't be the first time. I pack a few pairs of emergency undies in my handbag and wrap a jumper around my waist, just in case.

As I wait for the flight out of Zihuatanejo, with bacteria backflipping in my belly and brain, I think about the history of this beautiful and troubled state—the stories about shark attacks, and tourists inadvertently glancing the edges of cartel violence, and the fact that many local people live with a sense of constant, simmering caution. I think about how the birds piqued my curiosity and drew me right to the horizon's edge, until I pulled myself away, pulled myself to solid ground.

I feel as though I've gotten off lightly.

I can't wait to go back.

Oaxaca de Juárez

9.

On a Sunday evening, under umbrous old trees and the stone-cool shadow of a Spanish church, a band is playing. It's my first night in Oaxaca de Juárez, the capital city of Oaxaca state, which is directly to the east of Guerrero. I'm way up in the mountains, in the heart of the city at the central plaza. People of all ages have gathered to listen as the band plays covers of familiar songs by Buena Vista Social Club. Couples are dancing together gracefully, unselfconsciously. The black storm clouds flip open, loosing a flare of gold sun.

God, I feel sad.

Maybe it's the light, so soft, so different to the deadly, sun-drenched skies of Western Australia.

Maybe it's because we don't have this in our country, such open reverence for music, for dance.

Maybe I'm feeling sad about leaving Tom at home, feeling guilty for following the birds. He'll be over in a couple of months and I hope we can dance, clumsily, at the edge of a crowd just like this. I'll take him to the wine bar I found earlier today, the one with Spanish Tempranillo, and to the graphic design studios showcasing prints with skeletons and genetically modified corn, prints that seethe dark with the fear of disappearance. He'll bring a different perspective, will contemplate things I don't, notice the subtle details alluding to stories just beyond reach.

But he's not here, not yet.

An old man sees me brushing away tears. He offers his hand for a dance.

10.

'Every artwork casts a shadow,' Mexican artist and curator Francisco Guevara cautions me. Francisco is one of the directors at the artists' residency I'll be based at for the next month. He's talking within the context of Jean-Léon Gérôme's 1879 painting *The Snake Charmer* in which, perhaps unconsciously, the French painter asserts his own cultural fantasies and superiority. 'What shadow is your new novel casting?' Francisco asks.

Ultimately, Francisco is delivering a warning, a cautionary tale about the dangers of creating outside your own culture.

Unfortunately, my new novel is failing to cast much of a shadow at all. My characters have been playing up, especially my hero. Each syllable of each sentence is an effort to get on paper. I tell Francisco I'm not at the stage where I'm even thinking about shadows.

He nods and says that when you become aware of the shadows, when you swing to face them, to resolve them creatively, they disappear. But this swinging, this facing, this resolving, casts new shadows, at different angles, and it's impossible for art to exist without them.

I wonder if I was to write about some of the things I heard in Guerrero, what shadows would these stories cast? And I wonder about Mexican writers and artists, when they consider contemporary social issues in their art—does their work throw shadows too?

Later in the week, I visit the Oaxaca Textile Museum. An exhibition on the colour indigo, with textiles from Guatemala, China, Japan and West Africa, pulls me through the grand wooden doors. But what draws me back for two more visits is another exhibition, much smaller, titled *Bordando otros males*— Embroidering other evils. The artist, Miguel Hernández, is from the mountain town of Xalapa in Veracruz, formerly part of the Aztec Empire and ringed with cloud forests. I take a peek at the artworks—a bold blend of embroidery, watercolour and printmaking—before returning to the exhibition's introduction,

written by Lily Márquez Tamayo. She describes how drug
trafficking has shaped contemporary society and how people live
with constant needle-pricks of fear and are wounded by fear, so
much so that it restitches whole personalities, whole communities.
Lily asks the questions, 'When did this feeling start? When did we
allow narco-culture to enter our homes? When did I stop walking
in the streets for fear of being abducted?'[6]

As I wander through the exhibition, I take in the beating,
bleeding hearts in thread; the red skeletons stomping on each
other's backs; the T-shirts modelled on the three Greek goddesses
Clotho, Lachesis, and Atropos—the Moirai, responsible for
determining the length of a person's life and their quota of misery
and suffering. The T-shirts carry the words: *Desierto, Río bravo,
Violencia, Narcotráfico, Racismo ...*

The pieces in the exhibition I find most gripping are part of a
series titled *Fear.* Volcano-shaped people huddle under brilliantly
coloured blankets, indistinguishable but for a screaming mouth, a
frightened eye, limp hands. Maybe they're not blankets but body
bags. Both frightened and frightening, I'm getting the sense this
is real, this danger, this darkness, for many people in different
parts of the country. It's real and deeper and more complex than
I'd imagined. While it's impossible to guess what kind of shadows
such an exhibition might throw for future thinkers and artists,
what is clear to me in this moment is that the shadow of fear is
heavy, and in Mexico, it doesn't disappear when you turn to face it.

11.

The road up to my writing residency in San Pablo Etla passes
grocery stores, construction sites and hairdressers. Many of the
town's residents are indigenous Zapotec people, or 'cloud people',
for whom the ancient Mesoamerican city of Monte Albán once
formed an important social and political centre. The surrounding
valleys are filled with plots of corn, medicine gardens, home-based
paper factories, mezcal distilleries and sheds where naturally dyed
textiles are woven with backstrap or pedal looms.

It's a world from the embroidery of evil in the textile museum. Kids trip each other over on the way to school, a lady sluices water in front of a restaurant to dampen dust, the dogs laze on their bellies in the sun. I spend a lot of time listening to the dogs. In the nights the fights are savage. Packs of dogs, with wild, wretched barks, roll grenade-like down the mountain before exploding into full-on brawls. You can pick the losers the next day, the dogs with the bright rakes of blood on their snouts or bits missing from their ears.

While I feel restless in San Pablo Etla, Oaxaca de Juárez is only half an hour away. It's a city that continues to surprise and delight. I can walk the same street fifty times and see different things: a sign made from handpainted tiles, a dance group practising Cuban salsa, a Moorish-inspired garden of stone fountains and cacti.

My favourite place is the *zócalo* plaza. I spend hours throwing back gin and tonics and mooning over the music of the mariachi singers, who work their way along the bars one by one. Sometimes, the people at the tables around me join in, and the whole terrace swells with song. At other times, passers-by pause to listen, only to find themselves swept up in an impromptu dance.

One afternoon, with a storm hustling down the mountains in shades of black, I find myself walking toward a line of schoolgirls with blue ribbons in their hair and socks pulled up to their knees. They look maybe fifteen or sixteen and are led by a teacher, a young man dressed in a shirt, tie and long pants. The rain that's been threatening all afternoon begins to fall. Without breaking pace, the girls burst into song, spontaneously, in harmony. Their teacher catches my eye and beams. I grin back.

12.

In a valley not far from the residency, a mob of cannibals are licking their fingers over a grill of human limbs. A man fans the flames, fans an uncooked face atop a nest of burning wood. Another two men seem to be playing instruments—some kind of flute. I look closer. Oh, no. They're not blowing into bone; they're gnawing into bone. The cannibals are indigenous Mexican men and women, frozen in a primitive tableau imagined by Flemish-born Theodor de Bry in the 1500s. De Bry was famous for his engravings of the Americas—engravings exaggerated to exhilarate the European imagination, based solely on the tall tales of travellers and writers and missionaries.

He never actually set foot in the Americas.

But he also didn't shy from depicting tales of the atrocities committed by the Spanish conquistadors.

Over four hundred years later, Oaxacan artist Demián Flores has entered into a conversation with de Bry through his exhibition *América. Visiones nuevas desde el viejo mundo*. In English, it can be translated as *America. New visions from the old world*. Flores loads the cannibalism tableau, number three in the series *Antropofagia*, with additional connotations. The face in the flames? It isn't just any face, but that of *el Pozolero*, the one who cooks *pozole*—originally human meat, stewed for ceremonial purposes.[7] In our time, it's a reference to Santiago Meza López, a man believed to have dissolved around three hundred people in caustic acid at the bidding of the cartels.[8] Flores's print also references the forty-three missing students from Guerrero. *Nos faltan 43*. The fire becomes a symbol of the body-swallowing pyre that may have 'disappeared' the young men.

It's a haunting piece, in an exhibition that's utterly unsettling and thought-provoking.

I follow the birds—pre-Hispanic birds of ill omen—through the eighteen lithographs that make up the series *The Destruction of the Indies*. Here, we find ourselves confronted with the tremendous cruelties of colonisation: an infant ripped in half and offered to starving dogs, a row of people hanging from their necks, legs licked in flame. From de Bry's old visions, Flores creates a new hell, with both ancient and contemporary flourishes. The birds have been plucked from the *Codex Borbonicus*, an Aztec manuscript containing a divinatory almanac and a list of calendar celebrations. These birds were considered to carry out punishments, offerings and sacrifices for the gods. Then there are the Mayan archaeological structures, wrought in exquisite detail, and an effigy of Chalchiuhtlicue, the Aztec goddess of living water, bearing mute witness to the carnage below. We encounter former American president George Bush, who gazes not at the carnage around him but into middle distance, and Miguel Hidalgo, a leader in the Mexican War of Independence. Amidst this dense tangle of symbol one message becomes clear: the violence of colonisation by the Spanish has given rise to a more ferocious form of colonisation by organised crime and the state. While I'm thrilled by Flores's flair and ideas, he offers a wretched vision of contemporary Mexican society.

In the feathery presence of the birds of ill omen, it's a vision wholly without the promise of hope.

13.

Something happens when you've been out of the surf for a while. A heaviness comes over you, a sombreness, a low-level burn of depression. It's a feeling not even a gym workout, or a netball game, or a morning run through the cold Oaxacan mountains can lighten. When Tom and I were younger and still at uni, by the tenth day of a surfless east-coast spring, we had turned on country and on each other, bickering and nipping, until we realised our frustration was thanks to the dead-flat Pacific. Similarly, the comedown after a good swell can be savage. We'll mope about for days, struggling with the sharp absence of endorphins.

It must be tough to live with a surfer if you're not a surfer, to have to ride out our wild swings from adrenaline into misery and back.

My mum and sister know what that's like and they're getting in next week, ahead of a month together on Oaxaca's coast. It can't come soon enough. The mountains are playing tricks on my eyes. A distant ridgeline takes on the same smoky blue as a summer sea. My sleeps have turned salty, and when the sobbing of dogs doesn't jolt me awake, I dream of waves.

Tormenta tropical

14.

Playa Carrizalillo, close to Puerto Escondido on Oaxaca's coast, is eight hours from the city along a road that corkscrews through wild gardens of cacti, kapok and pines. It feels much longer. Our driver rally-races another minibus, despite an approaching blind corner. He plays cat-and-mouse with a young woman on a motorbike. He tailgates every vehicle we get close to. Another passenger, a local man, tells my sister Charlotte and I the driver is 'crazy'.

'There you go,' Charlotte says. 'Even the locals are scared!'

But my mum is unperturbed, cool as a cucumber in gin. 'I've been on worse buses in India,' she says, then goes back to looking out the window and listening to *Milkman* by Anna Burns.

We arrive at Playa Carrizalillo late in the afternoon. The air's turbid, clinging to our skin like a living thing after the thin, dry air of the mountains. We're staying up on a cliff overlooking tumbling palms, colourful bars, pina coladas and turquoise surf. This evening, some of the sets are so big the bay's shutting down completely. There's a left, packed with forty beginners on soft tops. Charlotte scoffs, says it looks like a heat in the 'kookie pro'. But there's also a right, breaking closer to the cliff, much steeper, and practically empty.

I surf the right that evening.

I can't wipe the smile from my face.

Three days later, a local surfer wipes it off for me.

15.

The sea's the off-white of old whalebone and I can still taste my morning coffee—strong beans from Chiapas. I'm alone. I love surfing alone. I always feel more in rhythm with the water, like I surf better, braver, more creatively.

This morning, I know where to sit for the deepest take-off, just on the other side of the boil. I know where to place my turns. And when three young local men paddle out, I know to greet them. I despise tourists at my own home break who can't offer a simple good morning.

'*Buenos días*,' I say, turning on my board and smiling.

They ignore me.

My words hang awkwardly.

That's when I should have gone in.

Usually, I'm a bottom feeder; I'll swing on anything, prefer quantity over quality. Tom's forever getting fed up with me, telling me to 'surf properly'. This morning, I surf properly, wait politely, and I finally line up a beauty, only to find Afro snaking me, paddling up on my inside, going for the wave as well.

I should have pulled back.

But I hate bad etiquette in the water. I know it's my turn. So, I go for it, I drop in on him, and we surf the wave together almost all the way to the beach. He flicks out and comes for me.

'Where are you from?' he asks in English.

'Western Australia,' I say.

'You should go back there. You should go back to Australia.'

'*Tranquilo*,' I say. Relax.

He sees red. He paddles closer. He's so angry, now, he can barely speak.

'You have no etiquette in Australia?' he asks. 'This is not your wave. Go home.'

That's when I should have considered if etiquette here is different; if locals get right of way, regardless of whether or not it's their turn.

Instead, I blow. I flip into the coarsest Spanish I know, a mix of vulgarities from both Mexico and Spain. I call the young man a motherfucker, a *pinche pendejo*, a coward, a pubic hair. I shout, furious, '*¡Que te folle un pez!*'—I hope you get fucked by a fish!

Then I swing for shore, a stream of invective behind me. The coconut sellers and the boys hiring surfboards on the beach stare as I walk past. I'm on the edge of tears. I'm disgusted with myself, ashamed all that elegance and style I aspire to in my surfing can be undone by a hot blaze of my own bad temper.

16.

It's not just me who's experienced localism at Playa Carizalillo. On TripAdvisor, Trustytraveler82 writes, 'On my first wave I got shouted at by one of the guides saying if I came close to the lesson again he would kill me.'[9] Nz_smarte recalls seeing a surf instructor drop in on a tourist and subsequently cop the tourist's board to his face. All of the instructors rallied together and demanded the tourist accompany the injured instructor to the hospital and pay for his stitches.[10]

The stories aren't just concentrated in this idyllic bay. I learn from other travelling surfers if you turn up to some spots on the Oaxaca coast without a Mexican surf guide (the going rate is about USD100 a day), you may be told to fuck off. If you don't fuck off, you may be threatened with a bashing, a tyre slashing, or a car torching. On one level, I understand the surf guide initiative. In rural places, where there's poverty, leveraging tourism to create jobs for local people makes a lot of sense. It's also a way to manage a resource sustainably. By enforcing an unofficial policy of 'no guide, no surf', local surfers can keep their line-ups uncrowded. On the other hand, it's the exclusivity thing again, the one that rubbed me the wrong way in Guerrero. It hurts—the idea of needing to pay someone serious money to access a resource that's free in most other parts of the world.

I'm in touch with the girls back home and I tell them about the way the young man at Playa Carizalillo intimidated me. My Ningaloo girlfriends are all surfers. I'm surprised when they're approving of his behaviour. You have to give it to him, they say. His abuse was effective. He got you out of the water.

And then, to my horror, they suggest we do the same.

We should tell the Chileans to fuck off back home, when they flood our local next winter.

17.

Most people wouldn't book a family holiday at a nudist beach. We're not like most people. I can be disastrously disorganised. When I was trolling the coast for a suitable Airbnb, I was fixated on finding a place close to raffish bars and reasonable surf. I didn't expect the three of us would be sipping our morning coffees while watching a naked man doing push-ups, another practising yoga, and a nude couple floundering in the shorey.

We're not prudes, no way. But we're picking up on something else about the vibe here at Playa Zipolite. An underdrift of drugs, a feeling that things could metamorphose—turn feverish.

'Where the fuck are we?'

Beyond the floundering couple, a left-hand rip bowl's running fast through the dancing water. I've had it to myself all morning.

'Well,' I say to Mum. 'It's sometimes called *la playa de los muertos*, the beach of the dead, because every year countless swimmers drown in the—'

'Yeah, but where are we?'

She means story. She means history. Later in the evening, Charlotte finds a thesis on tourism in the town, and she reads us sections off her phone. We learn it was a former hippie hangout, first visited by drifters in 1969, who walked five kilometres in on a dirt track to watch a total eclipse of the sun. In the early '70s, more travellers turned up, renting hammocks under *palapas*—open-air shacks—for a dollar a night. Beautiful naked women strolled the beach, there were no police, and drugs were readily available. As the decades clicked by, pot was subbed with heroin, dirt with pavers, kerosene with electricity. The foreigners remained a constant—they now account for about fifty percent of the local population—and so did the nudity.[11]

So, we know where we are. And in those first few days, we get a sense of the paradise those early travellers must have enjoyed. We welcome the sweeping, oyster shimmer of the ocean at dawn, and the peanut lady who visits our beachside table midmorning, with her cunning moon-shaped face and four missing front teeth. We welcome the afternoons, filled with hummingbirds and cold, white

Argentinian wine, and the evenings—especially the evenings, when the storms boil up over the ocean and the heat finally relents.

Then the metamorphosis begins.

It gets too hot to sleep. The fans aren't strong enough to cut through the mosquito nets. My sister and I are sharing a bed in the loft and one night, we wake with the violin-saw of mosquitos in our ears. We turn on the light and find four of them, circling fat on the inside of the net. They've bitten my knuckles. My sister has scratched her leg and left blood on the sheets.

We have a giggle at that.

The Airbnb host, an Italian woman, has already berated Charlotte for wearing fake tan to bed. 'It's not fake tan,' my sister clarified. 'It's bronzer!'

Downstairs, Mum's getting eaten alive as well. She's wondering why she's left her home in Broome for a holiday in a place where the heat and the mozzies are even worse. It's no ordinary heat: a *tormenta tropical*—a severe tropical storm—is brewing off the coast, and there are fears it will intensify into a hurricane.

In 1997, Hurricane Pauline nearly wiped Zipolite off the map.

18.

The swell picks up, swallowing the rip bowls and leaving only a big, shifting wedge in the corner. I get pitched from the lip on one and land bum-first on my fins. I scream underwater. My whole right cheek turns black. After that, I'm happy to bow out and watch the local bodyboarders throw themselves over the ledge of the wedge, with pit-hungry bravery.

On the night the hurricane's feared to hit, we bring the furniture inside, bolt the windows and stack our bags on the kitchen bench, in case the floor floods. Then we head off along a dirt track toward town for dinner. There's very little light, but we make out an owl in one of the trees above us. I've read the Zapotecs believed owls guarded the doors to the underworld ...

There's a rustle on the track behind us. A naked man has crept within a stone's throw. His phone illuminates his genitals.

'Mum,' I manage.

But Mum hasn't noticed, she's watching where she's putting her feet. He asks, in Spanish, if we would like love. Mum and Charlotte startle.

'*No gracias*,' I reply. '*Todo bien*.'

He shrugs, turns back, fades into black.

Mum reminds us of the naked showers we've been taking in the garden, asks how he knew we were leaving for dinner, suggests he's been watching.

On the main street, we sit at a brightly lit table. Men neck beers on the steps of the supermarket next door. An obese, white tourist rides up on a quad bike and inspects the menu, without getting off the bike. A European girl approaches, trafficking dreamcatchers. She's very thin, twitchy, perhaps tethered to one of the harder drugs on the street here.

We're mostly quiet at dinner.

Our organs, ankles and bellies all feel swollen with the heat. The fans bring no relief.

After seafood soup, we wander to a bar where rainbows drift the walls.

A young Israeli man comes in and says to the owner, 'Uh, is this a gay bar? Is it alright for me to be here?'

The owner, an American in flowing white robes, opens his arms expansively. 'Everyone's welcome here!' he says. 'Except assholes!'

That gets us laughing and when he brings us our second gin and tonic each for the night, we break our moody silence and ask about the naked man, if it's normal here, to be approached for sex on a dark backstreet.

'Absolutely not,' he says. 'Nudity on the beach is fine, but not on the streets. Wait just a moment!'

He takes off, leaving the bar unattended.

When he gets back, he proffers a whistle.

'If anyone comes near you, just blow. Go on. Give it a try!'

Mum's put in charge of the whistle. She sleeps with it under her pillow.

19.

'Tom's going to hate this,' Charlotte says, sipping from an icy margarita in a goblet.

We've left Zipolite behind after two days of blissfully cool rain—no hurricane—only to find ourselves sixty kilometres to the east in a place that's stranger still. We're in Santa Cruz, Huatulco, looking across the bay at cartel-owned condominiums, glancing over our shoulders at three tour buses, casting our minds down the road to the golf course and luxury resorts.

'Maybe you can blindfold Tom on the way from the airport?' Mum suggests.

'Maybe he'll be so buggered he'll sleep in the taxi?' Charlotte hopes.

No such luck. When Tom lands with his surfboards, flight-flattened curls and zonked eyes, the first thing he says after a kiss, is, 'Are we in some kind of resort?'

'Well ...'

In the 1980s, Fonatur, the Mexican government organisation responsible for developing tourism, expropriated more than 52,000 acres of prime coastal real estate. It built a town just off the coast—La Crucecita—and forcibly relocated fishing and farming families to make way for mega marinas and monster hotels. Fonatur representatives claim the organisation has learned from mistakes it made in Cancún and Ixtapa–Zihuatanejo, now factoring traffic congestion, pollution and waste management into its design. The area has an international Green Globe certification for being a sustainable tourism destination.

We're staying in a quirky, whitewashed hotel, catering mostly to local tourists. The pool, a venomous green, has been closed behind a skull-and-crossbones sign for days. On the upside, the staff are lovely, and we're proximate to the waves at Barra de la Cruz, Playa El Mojon and Majahual to the east, and to Puerto Escondido, Chacahua and Guerrero in the west.

So, after Tom shucks the jet lag, and Mum and Charlotte head on to New Orleans, we'll be in a good position to strike out in either direction. We'll be ready to start hunting those sand-bottom, right-hand barrels. We'll roll out our treasure map.

The Treasure Map

20.

On every surf trip there's a pot of gold. A wave that's difficult to get to. A wave mantled in stories of violence, danger and misadventure. A wave heavier than its busier neighbours.

We'll call it La Finca.

La Finca's on our treasure map of secret Oaxacan waves—a map gifted to us by a friend who spent six months scouring this exact coast. Our friend detailed the wind, swell and tide these waves need, but, unfortunately, conditions over the next week aren't aligning for La Finca.

So, we dip into another spot to the east of Huatulco, passing a carload of local surfers on the track in, who greet our grins with glares. Glares aside, it's a spot I like instantly for the old hotel on the waterfront. The hotel is peeling paint like burnt skin and it has a wild, out-of-season feel. No, it's not just an out-of-season feel, it's a never-been-in-season feel, a someone's-dream-turned-sour feel. I love places like this. My imagination scuttles up onto the wide, white balconies and takes a deep breath of heaving South Pacific air. I could stay here. Write a story here. Maybe an Aussie take on *The Shining*. A husband, wife and their small children move in to caretake an empty seaside hotel over a flat Mexican summer. The husband is balanced, content—the fishing's good, he likes the isolation. The wife's working on a new book. But, shit, it's not going well. Her characters have been playing up, especially her hero. Each syllable of each sentence is an effort to get on paper. And she's going mad with the lack of swell ...

'Mads! We're on! Are you coming?'

It's pumping. I'm a bit nervous. If anything, I'll go mad with fear over the excess of swell. I watch a chunky, right-hander jack up behind the rocks. It's a good shape. There are only two other surfers in the water. I've got my big board, the one I made myself. I'm almost superstitiously trustful of it. If I'm brave enough to go, it won't let me down, won't skid out at the bottom of a sucky one, or buck me onto dry reef. Okay. Okay, I've got this. Get out there, get three quick ones, and then decide if it's too much.

I take a deep breath and step into the surging sea.

21.

Clutching the map, we keep searching, pursuit is happiness. We travel by taxi through a valley of Mexican palmetto, through drifts of mosquitos, wicked as wasps. An old man edges a leathery horse to the side of the track as we pass. A Californian surfer sleeps on a cliff above an empty right-hand point break. He's roaming the coast by motorbike, surfing a single fin. We learn from him that on the last swell, the sand at Chacahua was perfect. Not a grain misplaced. A hollow, rushing right worthy of any Insta feed. There's another swell on the way, and despite the fact it'll be a bus, second bus, taxi, boat and a truck ride east from Huatulco, the promise of sand-bottom barrels is all the encouragement we need.

On the day we head off, I stick some money in my diary, in case we get robbed.

I shouldn't have bothered.

When we reach the edge of the Lagunas de Chacahua National Park, we get robbed anyway. Or, to be fair, we rob ourselves, by hiring a private *lancha* to take us through the mud-purpled lagoons. The boat hustlers convince us there's not another public boat until tomorrow morning, and with the swell filling in this evening, there's no way we'll risk missing the dawnie.

So, we're guided and glided through the meaty mangrove smell of swamplands, home to crocodiles and bioluminescent plankton, home to strikingly named birds: Inca doves, laughing gulls, and roseate spoonbills. What we spend on boat hire, we save on accommodation. For the first time in years, we haven't pre-booked.

Tom waits on the sand with our boards and bags, while I check out a few options—dim shacks with etiolated mozzie nets and time-humiliated mattresses.

I think about how the internet has completely shaped the way I travel. I no longer turn up in towns with a vague idea of where I might stay, or for how long. No longer move from place to place on a whim. Now, everything's predetermined. I imagine the things I've missed, the chance encounters, the way my trips might have quirked sideways, just a little.

This time, leaving something to chance pays off. I find a bright and breezy room for ten dollars a night, with river views at the back and ocean views at the front. There's no suggestion of swell just yet, but we set up on the front balcony, on plastic chairs, to keep an eye on it. A procession of people wander past toward the beach. We buy fresh oysters from two children, then steaming *tamales* from a woman whose features have an African cast. Chacahua was founded by runaway African slaves in the sixteenth century. Its isolation made it a perfect spot to hide, and it has remained one of the few strongholds of Afro-Mexican culture. In recent years, descendants from the slaves have been deported to Haiti and Honduras, with police asserting there are no black people in Mexico. But attitudes are shifting, and in 2015 the Mexican government included Afro-Mexicans in the national census for the first time.

As evening falls, I consider another Afro-Mexican connection, in literature. I've just started reading Juan Pablo Villalobos's *Fiesta en la madriguera—Down the Rabbit Hole*—in Spanish.[12] I can't read with much fluency, or without the help of a dictionary, but the fact it's in a second language slows me up, allows me to linger over the shape of each sentence, each image. The story's addictive as sugarcane, grisly and hilarious. It's narrated by Tochtli, the young son of a powerful drug cartel boss. More than anything, Tochtli wants a pygmy hippopotamus from Liberia for his private zoo. It becomes an obsession, one of several: samurais and sombreros, beheadings and bullets.

I rest the open book on my knee and reach down for the mozzie repellent. Next to me, Tom's nursing a beer, balls-deep in a Pelecanos: the one about the dogfights. I like this part of surf travel—the dawdling and dreaming between swells. I give my ankles a lick of the repellent. Out over the town square, someone reads an announcement. The PA's sound crackles, complicating the meaning. The town square consists of patchy grass and a volleyball net. A game's in full swing. Men drink beer in the violet shade of the palms.

I go back to my book.

Tochtli knows only fourteen or fifteen people, not including corpses. His view of the outside world is skewed by television. One evening, he watches a news report about a woman eaten alive by tigers at the zoo. They devoured everything but her left leg. He once asked his dad if he could visit the zoo. No way. Too dangerous. To compensate, his dad bought him a lion for a pet ...

Villalobos wrote *Fiesta en la madriguera* in Barcelona in 2006, when the online newspapers in Mexico were full of reports of mutilated bodies and severed heads. He says had he still been in his home country, he might have been reluctant to tackle drugs and violence in his fiction—so ever-present are these issues in everyday life. But the distance from Mexico allowed him to create a character like Tochtli, a boy who doesn't moralise, or judge.[13] *Fiesta en la madriguera* was penned for Villalobos' unborn son—he was compelled to give his son this 'poisoned gift called Mexico'.[14] For Tochtli, too, Mexico is a poisoned gift: '... *a veces México es un país nefasto, pero también a veces es un país magnífico*'[15]—sometimes Mexico is a dreadful country, but sometimes it's a magnificent country.

The next day, I get a taste of both, though once again, it has nothing to do with drug violence, and everything to do with the surf.

22.

The alarm goes off before the sun's first strafes. Chacahua works best on an incoming tide and it's just past low now. On an outgoing tide, it can be dangerous. The river to the right of the breakwall empties the lagoons, fans out, and pleats the wave with rips.

I'm fearful of river mouths.

On our honeymoon, I was swept out to sea. It was winter in Spain. Freezing. The tide at Mundaka was still draining. No-one else was stupid enough to be surfing. As soon as I skimmed off from the old stone steps, I knew I'd fucked it. I panic-paddled parallel to the snow-sheeted hills, trying to get out of the river's grip, frantic with self-talk: you've got a good wetty, you've had a coffee, the tide turns in two more hours, you can paddle for two hours no worries, the offshore's just like WA, and if you get stuck, Tom's there, he's watching, he'll call sea rescue …

But Tom wasn't watching. He was drinking a hot *cortado* in a harbour-side café.

I got dragged halfway to the offshore island. The day before, there were jetskis out there, towing surfers into a suicidal right-hander.

It took me over an hour to get to shore.

This morning, with a banana and butterflies in the belly, I fasten my leggie and look out to sea. It's the colour of steeped hibiscus petals.

'There's one!' says Tom. 'See that? Looked alright …'

Alright? It looked sublime—an empty right-hander rolling along a sandbar for four hundred metres.

We launch into the rip on our boards, duck dive to shiver off the sleep, then race each other out the back. Tom's in position first and he swings on the second wave of a set. I turn to watch. He explodes off the lip, fins out above the wave, water flying.

I love watching Tom surf—his style is distinct, an alloy of masculinity and grace. I spin back to the horizon and line up the next wave, take a few strokes, press my hands on the deck, arc into cobra, and then spring to my feet. I pump twice, before driving down toward the base of the wave, shifting my weight to my heels, opening my arms like the wings of a gull, then swinging the board vertically for the lip. Whack! I compress on the way back down.

The speed's like morphine. My feet now have a firmer purchase in the wax and my muscles' memory moves thoughtlessly: wings, swing, whack, compress.

Tom's paddling back out, grinning. But as we fall into pace together, we realise there's one thing missing that our treasure map had promised; there's no sign of those spinning, sand-bottom barrels.

23.

Four and a half hours later, my neck and back are in knots. It's not just from the surf, but from sleep, from the mattress and the rock-filled pillows. I'm desperate for a massage. In my early twenties I was too hyperactive to lie still for an hour on surf trips. Couldn't stand being touched. Couldn't stand wasting time. Preferred to be tearing around on my motorbike, or racing off for surf number three, coconut number four, coffee number five ...

Now, I reckon if I don't get these knots smoothed out I won't be able to move tomorrow, let alone surf. I leave Tom with Pelecanos and wander into the village. I pass signs warning of zika and tuberculosis. In a family compound at the edge of the river, I find a *curandera*—a traditional healer—who was born in Mexico City but married a man from Chacahua. Her English is perfect. She leads me to a wooden platform hanging over the river. It's screened by thin, white curtains. Every time a *lancha* passes, the water agitates, and the late-afternoon light refracts, as if through mosquito wings. The massage is good. Not enjoyable, it hurts like hell, but she's kneading all the right places.

When she finishes she says, 'You're a surfer. I can tell by where the knots are.'

Then she asks if I can do her a favour.

There's a young local surfer here. He's eighteen. He competes, he's the best in Chacahua. But six months ago, she gave him a massage, and he's claiming it fucked his back. Since then, he's lost comps. Hasn't been surfing well. Have I run into him?

'I don't think so ...'

'You would have remembered if you had. He likes getting into fights.'

Yesterday, she took her daughter to another toddler's birthday party. The young champion was there. He abused the *curandera*. Threw a glass of water over her blouse. The champion's mother watched. Said nothing.

'Oh my god,' I sympathise. 'I'm so sorry. You must feel terribly shaken.'

She went home to change, and then took her daughter back to the party. After the party, she reported the incident to the police. If the police do nothing, she says, then perhaps she'll fall back on the local village law. The champion's mother knows all about this—a vicious gossip, she once received a midnight visit from two men she'd been rubbishing.

They bashed her blue.

Jesus.

'So … what would you like me to do?'

'I want you to go to the loudspeaker, the one over the square, and tell the town what a great massage you've just had.'

24.

'Should have done it!' says Tom.

'She was using me,' I protest.

We're into November. It's the tail end of the south-swell season. While the wave at Chacahua's fun, it hasn't lit up as anticipated, and so, after a few days exploring some of the other breaks in the area, we pile into a truck out of there, bound for Puerto. On the outskirts of the village, the truck fills with young men with machetes. I apologise for our surfboards and get yarning with one of the boys in Spanish.

'Did you surf with the champion while you were here?' he asks.

'*Creo que no.*'

The young man's eyes shine with pride as he recounts the comps their local boy has won. He tells me of the magazines that have published stories about him. He's surprised I haven't heard of him in Australia.

We wind through a scorching drift of sand dunes, pass copses of prickly pear.

I think about our heroes. In the town where I live in Western Australia, it's not so different. We worship the men who charge the beefiest swells of winter, the men with the longest breath holds, the men with the largest following on social media. We worship barbeques and envy boats. We don't worship the immaterial, those who are compassionate, creative, thoughtful or generous.

The young man raps on the side of the truck with his knuckles and it slows.

'*¡Buen viaje!*' he says, as he climbs out with his friends. Then the four of them swing over a wooden fence and lope off into the cornfields to work.

25.

On the first *Día de muertos*—Day of the Dead—Tom's invited to climb into a giant skeleton puppet. Wearing his thongs from our IGA back home, he dances it down the street in a procession of hundreds of teenagers. Two brass bands play in competition, all trumpets and saxophones and trombones. The night's crackling, not just with lightning, but something else, perhaps the spirits of babies and children, who are visiting the families they've left behind.

We're staying in the backstreets of Puerto Escondido, above Playa Principal, a cove of seafood restaurants and *lanchas*. There's a puma skin pinned to the wall in the reception of our hotel and sketches of sombreros on the tiles in the bathroom.

The world-famous Zicatela isn't far from where we're staying. I still haven't paddled out. I took a good look at the memorial, which acknowledges the surfers who have drowned at the beach, then a good look at the wave, at the breath-compressing closeouts, and decided it wasn't for me.

Tom and I watched a moody, six-foot evening. A couple of local

Mexican girls in bikinis were pulling into some bombs. It was so far beyond my courage level I had no qualms just commentating from the bar, frosty margarita in hand. Tom, on the other hand, was restless in his seat, wondering whether or not to go back and get his board.

I'd been getting a bit pissed off at Tom. 'I'm hungry,' he'd say. 'I need a coconut. I need to wee. I need tacos. I need another coconut.' He'd been getting a bit pissed off at me. 'I need a margarita. I need a gin and tonic. I need to do some writing. Are the *tamales* gluten free?' The pissed-off-ness had nothing to do with these minor things and everything to do with the fact neither of us were getting those rumoured and effortless sand-bottom barrels.

And now, to add salt to insult, it'll be flat for the next three days.

So, when Tom sheds the skeleton, we'll be doing what normal, non-surfing couples do when they travel. We'll be heading for a romantic weekend on magic mushies in the mountains. At least, I hope it will be a romantic weekend. Once, after a shrivelly shake in Bali, my mozzie net turned into a wet, black mouth and tried to eat me alive.

26.

'How's the lack of a dunny seat for frosting up your freckle?' Tom calls from the bathroom. I laugh, and gaze out over a sea of pines where the mountains look like giant, stilled waves, and the rain floats, nudging ice. I buy a jumper from a group of women singing, '*Mira, mira, mira,*' and later, I find strands of a woman's hair knit together with the sheep's wool. We cast about for breaks in the cloud. Find a splash of sun in a timber café. Order hot chocolates. They're served in ceramic mugs and are superb—a mix of cocoa, cinnamon and almonds, whisked to a froth. We breakfast at the edge of a local soccer game, and the green salsa tacos burn in our bellies. Then we climb back up into the clouds to our hostel and order two serves of magic mushrooms from the front reception.

In deckchairs, we fall.

'Did you know,' I say to Tom, 'that in Cakchikel, an indigenous Mayan language, the word for poetry is *pach'un tzij*.[16] It means braid of words.'

'Yeah, right,' Tom says. 'How about these braids of clouds?'

Every so often, the braids come undone, sending light rippling down the valleys. I fight a strong urge to open my wings and take a running leap off the concrete roof. While the view's intensifying with every moment, it's also benign. Completely unlike home. At home, I look over a summer boneyard of sun-splintered pegs and a dead-limestone garden. I know if I go for a stroll in December, or January, without water, out past the boat and the wheelie bin, out over the spinifex country toward the snake canyons, I'd probably die.

'Only two weeks left,' Tom says.

We make a shrivelly-fuelled pact to rip ourselves in half chasing this next swell.

27.

It's after dark and Tom's nudging our rental car with its Yucatán numberplates down a dirt track toward Barra de la Cruz. Barra was the first of the Oaxacan point breaks to be exposed in the international surf media, and it's arguably one of the best right-hand point breaks in the world. The Rip Curl Search Pro held an event here in 2006, calling the wave La Jolla, a corruption of the Spanish *la joya*, which means 'the jewel'. The wave at Barra, which had been a closely guarded secret until then, blew up. Surfers flocked from all over the world for the dreamy right-hand barrels. But mass surf tourism brought the usual legion of problems to the indigenous village, and when the town council redirected the river, the sandbank supporting this perfect wave lost its magic.[17]

We've heard the sand is correcting and have decided to base ourselves here for the final two weeks of the trip.

Up ahead, there's something on the road, silhouetted in the headlights.

'What the fuck's that?' I sit up a little straighter in my seat.

'Looks like a rat,' Tom says.

We get closer.

It's ambling towards the car, a dinner-plate-shaped pool of darkness.

Oh my god. It's not a rat. It's a spider.

28.

I think about that spider as we walk, before dawn, to the point each morning. But my hunger for waves is fiercer than my fear. We're always the first to paddle out here. By the time I spot the head torches of the other early risers, a couple of French shredders, I've usually bagged two or three beauties, belted them all the way down the line. By seven, it's a shitshow of snakings, drop-ins and ditched boards. Tom doesn't mind working his way around the crowd at the top, but I struggle to hold my ground in a pack—prefer to move to the baby barrels on the inside. I surf with another couple of Aussies who refer to this section as the 'flare-up division', and we whoop each other in. I practise my backhand tube riding: work on keeping low, with my left knee down, right hand in the wall, and my white-knuckled left hand clutching the rail.

Every time I panic, look to escape, look to the beach, to the cameras, to the driftwood and palms, the lip of the wave chops my neck, back or board, and grinds me along the sand. On one spill, I graze half my bum cheek off. I come up breathless, anxious. But I tell myself to get back out there. Tell myself to try again. Tell myself to always be looking where I want to go, and to never be looking where I don't.

29.

Our eyes are still on the pot of gold: the wave heavier than its busier neighbours, the one almost impossible to find without a guide, the one you're not allowed to surf without a guide. We've got the spot pinned on Tom's phone. We've got the hire car. And our treasure map marks the exact, unmarked turn-off from the highway.

The search begins.

We feel the buck of rocks under the car's chassis. Hear the squeal of branches on the chrome. Get chased by a bull. We double back to a locked gate, with a sign that says, in emphatic typography: *NO TRESPASSING. PRIVATE PROPERTY.*

'The wave's on the other side of this gate,' says Tom.

I look at his phone and then shake my head.

'Does the treasure map say anything about a gate?' I ask.

'Nah, nothing.'

'I don't know, love. I don't really feel good about this. I mean, is it worth it—for a wave?'

Tom's silence offers an answer. Of course, it's worth it. This is the wave. The actual jewel.

'How about we leave the car here and walk for a bit, see what we see,' he reasons.

I reluctantly agree. We shoulder a backpack and slide our boards under the gate. The sun pours down like hot maize. A heavy thump of machinery can be heard up ahead. Before long, we find that the track is barred by another gate. This time, the sign warns of *perros locos*—crazy dogs. The machinery's louder now and there are shouts, too, of farmers, just out of eyesight, working a pawpaw plantation.

'I'll happily reason with a machete-wielding surf guide, or farmer,' Tom says. 'But *perros locos*? Fuck that …'

'Are we pulling the pin?'

'Maybe there's another way …'

For two hours, on foot, we follow cattle tracks and a single motorbike tyre deep into swampy long-grass country. A jungle cat stalks the distant ridgeline. A snake springs up at us. The trees bare themselves like throats, bristling with thorns. I'd read a book that suggested Mexico's thorny plants evoke the dead—evoke those ancient, herbivorous monsters that once roamed the forests and deserts.[18] The plants developed thorns as an evolutionary response to the monsters' teeth.

I'm still musing on thorns, when finally, the mangroves part to reveal the sandbank behind the wave. Tom high-fives me. We each have a swig of water. And then we realise our mistake. A crooked devil's horn of lagoon separates us from the sand. The green water's loaded with crocs.

The mythical wave is still out of reach.

Back at our *cabaña*, Tom loosens a tick. The graze on my bum throbs. We're both sunburnt. It's starting to feel like a real surf trip. And in the spirit of a real surf trip, we decide we have to brave up. At risk of dogs, machetes, guns, and feral surf guides—there's no way we're not going to surf this wave.

The stars on the forecast are aligning.

Monday, Tom's birthday, is shaping up to be the day of days.

30.

In the meantime, we keep searching, leaving before dawn, returning after dark. Between surfs, we eat along the highway, at *comedores* serving sinewy steaks, beans and rice. The food is simple, even when jazzed up with *salsa picante*, but the staff are relaxed and unfailingly courteous. Off the highway, we flog the rental. Hit tree roots and *topes* at speed, nearly flip it on a washaway.

So far, it hasn't let us down.

I'm bewitched by one particular point break, down one particularly tricky track. We turn up late in the afternoon. The air swims like honey and the light has a wistful, Australian east-coast summer feel. The beach sweeps from an abandoned lighthouse at one end to the granite shadows of mountains at the other. It's hard to judge how big the wave is from the fishing shacks where we park the car, but there's promising white water. We walk for about twenty minutes and paddle out into head-high waves that run for hundreds of metres, with sections that scoop out steep, and others that slow right up.

The potential is thrilling.

Sometimes, that's what you remember about a wave.

The potential, the furled possibility.

Later that night, a carload of Dutch boys said they'd surfed the same spot a few days earlier. They'd been told to fuck off by three American expats.

Later still, two coconut pina coladas deep, an Aussie chick says to us, 'You guys don't seem old. I mean, you're pretty cool, for y'know, like, how old you are.'

We've never imagined ourselves old.

We walk home together in thoughtful silence.

31.

The lock on the '*perros locos*' gate is only for show. When we stand on the other side, I half-expect dogs or gunshots. Nothing. Not even the sound of machinery. I slap my arm. It comes away wet with mosquitos and blood.

'Let's go, *vamos* ...'

This morning, we're three. Tom invited Noam, a young Israeli surfer, to join us for his birthday mission. Within a hundred metres, we encounter the first farmers.

'*Buenos días*,' we call.

'*Buenos días*,' they reply.

'*¿Qué tal?*'

'*Bien, bien ...*'

So far, so good.

We walk between rows of pawpaw plants toward the home-stead. As warned, here come the dogs. They're nothing like the dogs I'd imagined, all fanged and rolling with muscle. These poor creatures are gaunt and fearful. I rummage around in my bag for some biscuits and toss them into the grass. The dogs shy away. Alerted by the barking, a man has stepped out onto the homestead's balcony.

'*¡Buenos días!*'

He returns the greeting and then asks where our car is. We left it outside the farm, I tell him in Spanish. You don't have a guide? he asks. No guide, I say. He nods. And points along the track. The beach is another five or ten minutes.

'*Gracias*,' I say.

'*Gracias*,' the boys echo.

And then we're away, pretty much at a run, through a sticky

tunnel of dense vegetation. We wonder if anyone else has come down here this morning, if there's a surf guide here already, with guests from one of the Salina Cruz surf camps. The devil wind has been blowing its ring off for weeks, rendering a whole suite of point breaks unsurfable. What if there's a guide and it's pumping? What if we're threatened? What would happen if we went out anyway?

Up ahead, the carpark's empty. We can hear the surf. We crest the final sandy track. My stomach turns, Tom squeals, and Noam's eyes widen.

The ocean's a jewelled green in the morning light.

It's heaving. Stacked to the horizon. Luminous cylinders out the back slow into giant, grinding walls, then throw again, over white sand. There's no-one as far as the eye can see. No sound but the surf and the crying of gulls.

I'm scared shitless.

I get out for a quick panic paddle and then give up, cloak myself in a sarong on the beach and crouch behind the lens while the boys throw buckets.

They surf for five hours.

The memory card crams.

Just as we're gathering our things to go, four men turn up. Oh fuck. We share worried glances, then look back at the men. They're carrying fishing gear. After greeting us, the head fisherman says, very cordially, in Spanish, 'I'm sorry, but you can't be here without permission. Do you have a guide? No? Then I'm afraid you'll have to leave ...'

We all shake hands.

Back at the car, Tom clicks over the ignition and the whole dashboard blazes with alarm. He crawls under the car.

'We've fucked it,' he reports. 'We've crushed the oil sump.'

32.

One of the pawpaw farmers passes us on a lunchtime beer run. We hitch a lift to a mechanic, buy four bottles of oil, and then nurse the rental back to Barra. That evening, the taco bar's packed with surfers—Noam, the Dutchies, the flare-up division Aussies. Tom throws down 1,500 pesos, turns to the room, and declares it's his thirty-fifth birthday and, as such, there'll be free drinks for everyone until the tab runs dry.

33.

It's my last surf in Mexico. I can't see a thing in the dark. The moon has set and there's only a cold foam of stars over the hills. But as I paddle out, I can see my hands. They're dancing with biolumi-nescence. Or rather, the movement is dancing and it's a disconcerting feeling, seeing movement take form beyond my skin.

Yesterday evening, we were reflecting on barrel riding.

'When I'm in there, like, when I was in *that* barrel ...' Tom's referring to his wave of the winter last year, a five-foot drainer, so scary he could've cracked pistachios between his bum cheeks. 'When I was in there, all I wanted was to get the fuck out. Then, the second I was spat out, I wanted to be back in.'

I think I understand what he means. I've locked into a few now, on the inside, and the wave has pitched in front of me, canting the world in a slightly different way. There's something exhilarating and terrifying about being tucked so close to such power ...

I shake free from my thoughts, see a darker smudge on the horizon.

'Are you on this, love?' I shout.

'Nah, all yours,' Tom shouts back.

I swing for it, blind, and take off. I have just enough time to adjust my feet, when I feel the wave speeding up, dropping out, becoming hollow. I compress, grip my left rail. My right fingers—sparkling—drift the wall. I forget to breathe. The wave's curling, cocooning me in aquatic stars. I don't look to the beach, to the head torches of the Frenchies, to the driftwood or the black silhouettes of the palms. I look into perfect stillness, perfect presence.

And then I'm clamped and cartwheeled in the perfect wipeout, a thousand gannets and white terns and shearwaters beating in my breast.

The Sea-affected Life
Mark Smith

From its ancient beginnings in Hawaii, surfing has grown into a billion-dollar business worldwide. Surf brands are listed on stock exchanges, the World Surf League streams contests into our loungerooms, boards are mass-produced in Asian factories, and webcams and online updates keep us informed on the conditions along our chosen stretch of coast. And yet, every day, surfers stand with boards under their arms looking seaward, sand or rock or concrete under their feet, reading the waves for size and shape and speed. They squint into the sun or peer through the gloom, feeling for an offshore at their backs. The larger world of surfing means nothing when they duck dive under the shore break, leap off the end of a rocky point or stroke out into a fast-moving channel. There are no pros in the line-up, just a collection of like-minded men and women hoping to snag a few waves before work or in the middle of the day, or chasing the elusive late-afternoon glass-off. They may be doctors or teachers, builders or baristas, plumbers or musicians, but they all live sea-affected lives, attached in some intrinsic way to a coast they call home.

Photographer and filmmaker Mick Sowry, writer Favel Parrett and musician and artist Jeff Raglus all live on Victoria's Surf Coast. The art they create has been shaped and influenced by their love of this coast and their connection with the water. And in turn, they have touched the lives of others through the stories they have told on film, in novels, in songs and paintings. The courses of their lives have twisted and turned, at times pulling them away from the sea, but they have always found their way back home.

The west coast of Victoria took shape when sea levels rose at the end of the last ice age. The Bassian Plain connecting Tasmania to the mainland was flooded and the coastline west of what is now known as Port Phillip Heads formed as a succession of long sandy beaches and crumbling limestone cliffs. For tens of thousands of years prior to white settlement, Indigenous people fished, hunted and thrived along the coast and hinterland. The Wadawurrung people populated the Bellarine Peninsula and the rivers, beaches and estuaries west to the Painkalac Creek at Aireys Inlet. Past the Painkalac, taking in much of the Otway Ranges, was Gadubanud country. The area is dotted with middens bearing witness to large encampments on high points overlooking the reefs, where people once feasted on shellfish, waterbirds and wallabies.

The relative shallowness of the adjacent Bass Strait, the proliferation of reefs jutting out below rocky points and its geographical exposure to swell all combine to create a coastline with a wide range of surfable waves. There are iconic surf breaks here, like Bells and Winki, but locals are also drawn to the lesser known, more remote reefs further south. Past Cape Otway, where the forest grows to the shoreline, unbroken swells formed by storms deep in the Southern Ocean meet land for the first time. These waves aren't for the faint-hearted—just getting to them can be an adventure in itself. Worn tracks through forests lead to rugged cliffs and goat tracks wind down to small bays that provide access to the surf beyond.

Surfers who call the west coast home are as likely to measure the seasons by the wetsuit they wear as by the calendar. The three/two covers much of spring and autumn, the four/three the cold days from June to September, while the two/two sees them through the warmest months. While the coast has a reputation for big waves, particularly in winter, there is an equal number of benign days, especially in the period from October through to April. Climate change is affecting the seasonal patterns, the temperature of the water and consistency of wind direction. The water is staying warmer through to May, and large east-coast lows are pushing further south, bringing tropical heat into the previously dry summers.

The demographic of surfers on the west coast has also changed enormously in the last two decades. Torquay, with its variety of reefs and beach breaks, is only an hour and a half from Melbourne and the plain stretching north towards Geelong is rapidly filling with housing estates. The weight of numbers falls heavily on breaks like Winki and Bells. While they don't yet host the sorts of crowds that Snapper Rocks or The Pass attract, a good day will see sixty surfers in the line-up. It is a long way from the isolated and uncrowded days before Torquay established itself as the home of surfing in Australia.

This is the coast Mick, Favel and Jeff call home. The art they create is shaped by their daily rituals, their time in the water, their knowledge of the reefs, points and beaches, and their determination to protect them. Their creative practices have taken them around the world—from Portugal to Hawaii, Denmark to Scotland, Antarctica to Ningaloo Reef—and brought them a fair measure of success and recognition. Their individual stories are unique, their forms of artistic expression varied, but they share the common language of the sea-affected life, of surfing and exploring and interpreting what they see in pictures and words and music. They have seen the transformation of coastal life and, while they may yearn for a simpler time, they value the surfing community of which they are a part. It is still strong in the line-up at Bells, where Mick feels most at home, Torquay Point, where Favel regularly paddles out in the pre-dawn gloom, or on one of the banks Jeff enjoys further west. The ocean has formed the backdrop to their lives, nourishing and sustaining them, helping them celebrate and grieve, and firing their imaginations.

Mick Sowry saw his first surfboard in 1959. Holding his father's hand, he was standing at the front gate of their house at Henley Beach in Adelaide. The board was strapped to the racks of an FB Holden station wagon and he thought it looked like a rocket. He didn't know anything about surfing but from the moment he saw that board, he wanted one. That awe-struck five-year-old boy had no inkling of the way surfing would shape his life, take him around the world—from Nazaré in Portugal to Waimea in Hawaii—or that it would lead to him settling on Victoria's Surf Coast.

The ocean had entered his bloodstream by osmosis. Family legend had it that his father had dropped him into a rockpool in Fiji when he was just eighteen months old. It was 1955 and family pictures show the blue bathers and T-shirt he was wearing. The story goes that he nearly drowned.

Their house at Henley Beach was a hundred metres from the water and that beach was Mick's earliest introduction to the power of the ocean. He delighted in sitting in the stormy shore break and letting the waves pound him, ragdolling him across the sand. Finding his feet, he'd launch himself at the next wave, only to be picked up again and deposited up the beach. He still considers it the most glorious thing he's ever felt. He learned to swim through imitation, teaching himself by watching others at the beach. Before long he was diving to pick up rocks on the sandy bottom and running with them for as long as he could hold his breath. The image of all those adult legs kicking in the water is imprinted on his memory.

Television arrived in Australia in time for the Melbourne Olympics in 1956. Mick's parents got a black-and-white set around this time and he vividly remembers seeing the first vision of surfers riding Waimea Bay. Thirty years later, he would ride Waimea, in his own mind completing a circle back to that grainy footage he watched at the family house in Henley.

Today, Mick's face shows the weathering of a man who should never have been a surfer. The freckle-faced kid with Celtic skin who was perpetually sunburnt, and who endured the ignominy of being lathered in calamine lotion night after night, is now a man in his sixties. There are stories in the deep lines that spread from the corners of his eyes when he smiles, his greying hair and beard adding to the wizened 'old man and the sea' vibe. The smile comes readily, though life has been hard on him in recent years. You get the sense he wants to tell his story, not for selfish reasons but to try to place the events of his life in some sort of order so he too can understand how he got here in one piece. We all interpret our own journeys but there's a certain amount of self-censorship determined by ego. When I meet Mick to discuss this story, he's quick to set the rules: nothing is off limits.

In 1964, Mick's family moved from Adelaide to bayside Mentone, in Melbourne. Again, they lived close to the water, on Beach Road, but this was different to Henley. The suburbs of Melbourne hugged the curve of Port Phillip Bay and, in the early '60s, Mentone was a nest of tea-tree-lined dirt roads wedged between Nepean Highway and the coast. Horseshoe-shaped, the bay has 260 kilometres of coastline, but no surf. It is largely enclosed water, protected from the ocean swell by two peninsulas that come within three kilometres of meeting at Port Phillip Heads.

Who doesn't remember every detail of the first time they stood up on a surfboard? For lifelong surfers that day is imprinted on their soul—the break, the weather, the make and dimensions of the board. Mick's first surf was on a holiday back to Adelaide, visiting his best friend from his days living there. He was two and a half months shy of fifteen. At Moana Beach he rode his friend's brother's V-bottom George Rice. In his recollections of that day, he's sure he found his feet quickly, as though this was something his body had been waiting for since birth, and was trimming the wave by the end of the session. Now, he thinks they were probably three- or four-foot waves, though to his fevered young mind in 1964 they had eight-foot faces. He loved every minute of it, but he paid dearly for having spent most of the day in the water. His pale skin betrayed him again. He was severely sunburnt, blistered and suffering sunstroke. But the pain did nothing to diminish the glow of the day, the feeling of the old George Rice under his feet, the *slap-slap* as it trimmed across the face, the awakening of endorphins that would become the addiction of a lifetime.

Back in Mentone, when the south-westerly sprang up and

the bay turned to a cauldron of whitecaps, Mick surfed the wind swells on a borrowed board with his neighbours and schoolmates. His connection with the water grew. When he wasn't surfing, he'd be swimming or snorkelling over the reefs that dotted that part of the coast.

There were two establishments that dominated the foreshore at Mentone: the wedge-shaped edifice of the Edgewater Hotel and, on the sloping land opposite, the blunt brick-and-glass buildings of St Bede's College. The De La Salle Brothers were charged with the responsibility of educating the boys of the many Catholic families that populated the area. Mick remembers classes of sixty-five kids in year seven. The brothers held sway with liberal use of the strap but, in Mick's mind, engendered no great love of learning in the process. He was a daydreamer and underperformed academically. It wasn't that he didn't like learning—his biggest issue was that he was interested in everything.

On New Year's Day, 1970, exactly two months before his sixteenth birthday, Mick bought his first board—a seven-two Fred Pyke—from Parkview Marine in East Brighton. He continued surfing the bay but eventually he and his mates found their way to the genuine surf breaks that dotted the exposed coast of the Mornington Peninsula. To Melbourne surfers, it was the east coast, given it stretched east from Port Phillip Heads. Mick liked the open ocean beaches around Gunnamatta and the reefs closer to Westernport Bay. Still a teenager, he travelled down with older neighbours. He became one of the founding members of the Peninsula Surfriders Club and, though he never felt comfortable competing, managed to reach State A Grade.

It was during these years he realised his relationship with the sea was different from most of his friends. The reason he believes he didn't compete well was because of his self-consciousness. He was acutely aware he didn't fit the norm physically or mentally. His dark, curly hair would never go blond and his pale skin would never go brown. 'That self-consciousness is something that colours my whole life,' he says now. 'As a kid, it was a self-esteem thing, but

I was also a visually sensitive person. There was an aesthetic in surfing that I wanted to meet stylistically. But there's always been a part of me that just wants to sit out the back and gaze into space.' He made sense of life through being in the water. It was his fallback position, the place he could go to sit and stare and dream and plan.

Before long, Mick discovered the west coast and was immediately drawn to the power of the waves around Bells and Winki. This connection would become a lifelong attachment. He loved the size of the waves, the sense of adventure they inspired in his young heart. Eventually he would find his way down south to the wild stretch of coast between Cape Otway and Port Campbell. The more epic the adventure, the better, whether it was climbing down a cliff face or paddling out through a keyhole.

Mick had aspirations to travel, a yearning that deeply affected his life because it took him away from formal education. He was a voracious reader, interested in everything, but as he entered his final years of schooling he couldn't decide on a career. Surfing was a distraction that affected study and commitment in his first attempt at year twelve. He failed, having even gone surfing on exam days. He repeated the year, passed well enough, applied and was accepted into industrial design at RMIT. His application had included an art ability test, which he did while working on a tin mine in Tasmania as a powder monkey. The tin mine jobs were an annual school holiday thing—they bought him a new surfboard every year—and included stints as a seismic survey assistant, a house painter, a general labourer, and even an armed guard. He stayed four years at RMIT, moving from industrial to graphic design, before leaving without graduating to go into advertising.

Mick's career in advertising would span thirty years. Being relentlessly curious, he had the ability to assimilate information from any brief and to creatively communicate ideas for a given market. In many ways it satiated his need for creative expression, but he still thinks his best work was so obtuse no-one else got it. While he made a good living at it, the facile nature of the advertising industry ground him down. In many ways it was the antithesis of everything he yearned for and found, partly, in surfing. It wasn't soulless work, but it fed a consumerism he struggled to believe in.

Based in Melbourne, his love affair with the Victorian coast grew and through it he came to understand more about himself and what the water gave back to him. Trips became more than just a drive and a surf—they became journeys. He surfed a lot on his own and revelled in the drive home, stopping and taking photos, often finding the longest route to prolong the adventure. He liked the inner journey of being by himself, thinking and exploring, the great mystery of hunting for and finding new breaks.

In 1978 Mick headed to Europe with a mate, Rene Johnson. He'd been surfing seriously since leaving school but there were greater adventures to be found in France, Spain and Portugal. Mick believes they were among the first Australians to surf Hossegor in the French Basque country, after Paul Witzig visited there with Wayne Lynch, Nat Young and Ted Spencer to film the seminal surf movie *Evolution* in 1969. And then there was Nazaré in Portugal at twelve to fifteen feet, the biggest waves he'd ever surfed. Their leg-ropes broke virtually daily but they'd mend them over their camp stove and paddle out again straight away.

Later in that trip, Mick and Rene flew to Hawaii, determined to ride the waves they'd dreamed about since poring over them in surf mags as kids. But for Mick it all came to naught. He caught influenza and that part of an incredible year was wasted. He wouldn't return until the late '80s, finally fulfilling his ambition to surf Waimea.

Mick is very hard to ruffle, and he brings a sense of calm to surfing big waves. By his own admission, he doesn't have a panic button. The Nazaré experience was challenging, but he always had a plan and confidence in his ability to get in if things went pear-shaped. He has never been fearful of the sea. Maybe it all stems from that Henley Beach shore break, being happily belted up the beach time and time again as a five-year-old. That's not to say there haven't been close calls over the years. He vividly remembers a two-wave hold-down in 1991 at Two Mile on the far west coast. Big-wave specialist Ross Clarke-Jones famously goes to his happy place, the disco, when he's dealing with a long hold-down and Mick does something similar. But that day at Two Mile he was lucky. As the second wave grabbed hold of him and drew him up inside its face, his head popped out through the lip long enough for him to get a breath before he was driven back under.

One day in 1984, while still working in Melbourne, he came back from a surf and dropped in on a mate, Chris Copping—the bass player and organist in Procol Harum—at his house in Albert Park. There was an English girl sitting in the backyard, a girl so beautiful Mick thought he'd never have a chance with her. Her name was Sue Coley and twelve weeks later they were engaged. Sue had been born in South Yemen to British Air Force and Navy parents, spent her early years in Kenya and spoke Swahili until the age of seven.

Mick and Sue began a life together, and had two sons, Joey in 1992, and Tomas in 1995, while Mick continued his career in advertising. Surfing kept him in touch with the water and his network of friends, including Wayne Lynch and Nat Young, continued to grow. Caught up in the world of advertising, Mick felt discontent brewing. In the back of his mind he'd always wanted to be an artist, to express himself creatively in a way that didn't involve convincing someone to buy something.

Mick loved Paul Witzig's film *Evolution*. Through the 1960s Witzig charted the changes in surfing as longboards gave way to shortboards. Mick had developed his own filmmaking skills through advertising, though he had never made or directed anything like a major film. But his will to move into a different creative space led him to sell his house, with Sue's blessing, to finance a film about surfing, a revisiting of *Evolution*, some forty years later.

As anyone involved in film knows, most of the hard work is done before a single scene is shot. The financing, logistics, personnel and locations, all were new to Mick. Three years of development went into the film idea before he approached Richard Tognetti of the Australian Chamber Orchestra in 2007 to do the sound design. Richard counteroffered by asking Mick to help him on a project called *Musica Surfica*. A keen boardrider himself, Richard wanted to film a different sort of surfing, finless surfing, and get young bums on seats at classical music concerts. Why finless? Richard's friend Derek Hynd was surfing finless boards and he wanted to show people the benefits of risk, in learning and life. 'The finless surfing is a metaphor for everything we do,' Richard told Mick. 'We want to take people out of their comfort zone.' Mick wrote a treatment for a documentary that was sent to the head of Foxtel, Kim Williams, who loved the idea. And so *Musica Surfica*, the concert series and film was born.

Four months later, in May 2007, Mick and his crew boarded flights to King Island in the middle of Bass Strait, halfway between Victoria and Tasmania. The surfers who came with him included Tom Carroll, Derek Hynd and master shaper Tom Wegener, as well as Jed Done, Sage Joske, Heath Joske, Dane Beevor, Belinda Baggs, Dane Peterson and Warren Pfeiffer. Some of the boards they rode were ancient Hawaiian designs, while others were more modern. The musicians also went along for the ride, the surfing members of the ACO included, and they performed for locals during the two-week shoot.

Watching *Musica Surfica* transports the viewer into a stunning, isolated location. Tognetti described the film as the meeting of two forces, so-called high art and surfing. The cinematography captured the beautiful bleakness of King Island, windswept and populated by farmers and fishermen. The surfing was sublime, and the adventure of what they were doing was etched into the faces of the surfers and musicians.

For a film developed around such an abstract concept, one made on a shoestring budget and filmed by an effective novice, *Musica Surfica* was very successful. It was sold to the ABC, shown on Foxtel and toured the world's film festivals, winning best film at the New York Surf Film Festival, best adventure film at the San Francisco Ocean Film Festival and best film and soundtrack at the French International Surf Film Festival. It also screened at festivals in Brazil and South Africa.

For Mick, his great yearning for artistic expression had found an outlet. This idea that had been stewing in the back of his mind since he was a teenager, that he needed to find a way of interpreting life through art, had finally come to fruition. He was later invited by the ACO to write, produce, direct and coedit another film, a major performance work for film and orchestra entitled *The Reef*. The location this time was Gnaraloo Station, on the tip of Ningaloo Reef in Western Australia. Derek Hynd, Ryan Burch, Dane and Tully Beevor, and Taylor Miller were featured. The crew included cinematographers Jon Frank and Edward Saltau, photographer Ed Sloane and composer Iain Grandage. A strong Indigenous element was infused into the music by Mark Atkins and Stephen Pigram. They shot hundreds of hours of footage that Mick and Jon Frank edited into one seamless day, structured as a metaphoric life, from birth, underwater before dawn, to death, as the Milky Way blinked out slowly in a vast desert sky.

The Reef transcended expectations of what a film involving surfing could be. Each piece of music told a different story about life, most of it in the water but others, like Pigram's beautiful, haunting 'Mimi', performed in front of projections of vivid desert landscapes.

The surfing was timeless. In an interview with Swellnet, Mick said, 'Surfing, in this sense, helps you get an essence of the music and express that essence visually. It is the dance. In my mind, the surfing, in *The Reef*, is a representation of being the best you can be as a human ... But it's not really about the surfing, it's about life, grace, resignation and contentment.'[1]

The Reef was performed around the world and won the Surf Culture Award at the 2013 Australian Surfing Hall of Fame Awards.

In 2014, Mick threw himself into another venture with two mates, Mark Willett and Jock Serong—a high-end magazine called

Great Ocean Quarterly. Mick says they wanted to create something that connected everybody with what he called the sea-affected life. It was about art and literature with a watery, oceanic twist. Though they were encouraged by a close friend of Mick's, Andrew Jaspan, then the editor of the *Age*, to go digital at a time when the market was becoming very difficult for print-only magazines, they stuck with their plans and produced seven editions of *GOQ* before the bills stacked up too high. They paid every one of their debts before they had to abandon the project. Mick maintains he has no regrets, though he poured himself into the design, building and even some writing of the magazine, regularly working fourteen-hour days. The project lasted three years and each edition was a work of art, with articles from around the world encompassing everything from ecology to Fred Williams paintings of the Bass Strait islands, from the stunning underwater photography of David Doubilet to music sessions in tiny country halls called Church of the Open Sky.

Following the demise of *Great Ocean Quarterly*, Mick was invited to do a redux of *The Reef*, a grander revision that was shown with acclaim at Walt Disney Concert Hall in Los Angeles, 92Y in New York and later, in early 2017, at the Barbican in London.

But even successful art doesn't always pay the bills. All these adventures took a toll on the family financially. The self-funding of projects from their life savings, along with living and school expenses for the kids, led to Mick and Sue losing almost everything. Having always been attracted to the west coast of Victoria, Mick moved his young family to Torquay, still dipping in and out of advertising work to stay afloat, while continuing to explore his own photography and writing.

Reflecting on those years, Mick reckons all artistic endeavours operate on the margins. They are often costly, and the rewards are rarely financial in nature. And when reality came pounding on the door, demanding payment, payment was made, but the surf remained as he and Sue rebuilt their life. It kept him centred and strong, and things began to improve. From his home break at Bells to the big reefs down south, he continued to find inspiration and solace in the water, no more essentially than when his wife, his life partner, his best friend, Sue, passed away from pancreatic cancer on 18 January 2019.

Sue battled her cancer for just five months. Every minute he wasn't working, Mick spent with her, from diagnosis onwards. Sue ran a small cleaning business and with her illness, Mick took it over. The relentless pain-management routine and the effects of chemo nearly killed Sue within eight weeks. This was followed by time in palliative care, a period Mick views as some of their best days together. He slept on a chair next to her bed for seven weeks in total. 'We always loved, but we fell in love again,' he says. He only surfed when Sue sent him away. She knew he needed the recharge it gave him. For Mick it was a place to re-energise and go back into the fight, the fight to keep his own sanity while watching someone he loved so much die. 'Everyone says you should meditate,' Mick says, 'and that's what I do, out the back at Bells, watching the horizon.' During that time, surfing wasn't an escape, just a place where he wasn't thinking as much about the worst thing in his life.

When Sue passed away, it took a while for Mick to find the ocean again. Grief can't be hurried, and he struggled to comprehend life without her. But the day came when he threw his board into the car and headed for Bells. He told one friend what he was doing but by the time he pulled off his first wave there were a dozen paddling out. A mate threw himself off his board and hugged him. Out the back, they floated and talked. Friends slipped off their boards to hold him. The water held him. Mick had been taken aback by the attendance at Sue's funeral, people he hardly knew who'd shown up to both mourn and support. Now, out in the water at Bells, there was the added blessing of friendship through a shared connection with that place, and with what it meant to Mick.

Like many of us, Mick's life is an arc that encompasses love and mystery and grief and adventure. And, for him, the sea has been central to it all. 'Out in the water, you're still young,' he says. 'The shoreline in Victoria—thanks to those who have worked hard to preserve it—is still pretty much the same as when I was sixteen. The ocean is my constant and surfing is what I do there. It is one of the most important threads in my life. My family is first, always. My love of humanity and my faith in it follows, and my need to communicate the beauty and value of the environment stems from that'.

You get the sense when you sit down with Mick that the kid getting belted across the sand in the Henley Beach shore break is still there. Like the five-year-old who thought the boards on the top of that old FB Holden were rockets, the sense of wonder still thrives in an older, wiser body.

Most of Favel Parrett's writing days begin in the same way: waking before dawn, brewing a coffee, pulling on her wetsuit, driving to Torquay Point and paddling out as soon as it's light enough to see. Through surfing she has developed a deep love and respect for the ocean and it features heavily in her first two novels, *Past the Shallows* and *When the Night Comes*. But her first memory of the sea fills her with dread. She was six years old and her family was moving to Hobart, travelling on the *Princess of Tasmania*, the ferry that crossed Bass Strait between Melbourne and Devonport.

Bass Strait is a notorious stretch of water, principally due to its shallowness. It covers what was once the land bridge that connected Tasmania to the mainland. The entrance to the Strait from the west was called 'The Eye of the Needle' by the sea captains plying the great southern route to Australia from England in the nineteenth century. They would drop as far south as they dared to find the Roaring Forties, the gales that wrapped around the globe just north of the sea ice, then make the run for the entrance to the Strait between Cape Otway and King Island. The wrecks that litter the west coast of Victoria bear witness to the difficulty of threading that needle.

When Favel, her brother and mother boarded the *Princess of Tasmania*, they were advised to go straight to bed as a rough crossing was anticipated. Down in the bowels of the ship where the tiny, windowless cabins couldn't hold out the stench of diesel, Favel was seasick and terrified. She remembers thinking she never wanted anything to do with this thing, the ocean.

Settled in Hobart, Favel caught the small ferry across the Derwent River to school in Bellerive every day. She waited on the jetty in the rain, often in the cold and dark, watching the mystery of the river. The Derwent is tidal and the ride to school was often rough, the little boat buffeted by whitecaps when the southerly blew up from Antarctica. These journeys reinforced everything she thought about the sea—that it wasn't a place for her.

On top of her aversion to the water, Favel was a red-headed, pale-skinned girl, so even when the sun came out and everyone else was having fun, she'd be under a tree, wearing a hat. For twenty-seven years she believed the beach life wasn't for her. Then she discovered surfing.

On a trip to Byron Bay, her brother, James, had had a surf lesson. When he returned to Victoria, where Favel had been living since she was sixteen, he convinced her to try surfing, thinking she would love it. Favel was sceptical. What could surfing possibly offer her? She still equated the water with hot days sheltering under beach umbrellas and plastering herself with sunscreen. But James persisted and eventually coaxed her into the water at Jan Juc, near Torquay. It was winter and to Favel's surprise she loved the feeling of being in the surf. It was something new and unique and unexpected. She realised for the first time you didn't need to be a beach person to enjoy the water. It was the wildness that reached out and touched her, the feeling of the cold and the depth, the way the ocean swayed under her, the way she moved on top of it. It was a love affair born of grey skies and forbidding shorelines and it connected with her deep sense of the wild. For years she'd loved the forests and the wildlife of the west coast, and now she was able to view the ocean through similar eyes. That first experience in the surf at Jan Juc began a connection with the Southern Ocean, a connection that would find its way into her writing and lead to her award-winning first novel, *Past the Shallows*.

Favel wasn't strong academically. She confesses to being a remedial English student. She was a slow reader and maintains she still struggles with spelling and grammar. But in year twelve, a librarian at her school recommended *Wuthering Heights* and, in much the same way she would later find the sea, she discovered what books could be. When she finished school, she continued her reading habits and threw herself into writing and printing her own zines. She loved the zine community, the buzz of interviewing bands, writing stories then photocopying and distributing her work. But, at some point, she decided writing wasn't for her. It was all too hard, and she gave it away for twenty years.

As Favel moved through a series of evermore uninteresting, short-term jobs in Melbourne, surfing took hold of her and she found herself drawn to the water more often. Then, her life's path swerved again when her grandmother died and left her and James a substantial inheritance. Never having had this sort of money in their lives, they were determined to use it wisely. It was James who came up with the plan to buy a shack in Torquay, convincing Favel they could now stay down the coast more regularly rather than facing the drive back to Melbourne every time they went for a surf.

Favel is convinced she never could have written *Past the Shallows* if she wasn't surfing. In her words, it gave her the language of the water. She became a regular at Torquay Point, making friends and finding her way into the surfing community. She yearned for a sense of belonging, and found it in the line-up with everyone from teenagers to eighty-year-olds.

Favel returned to writing through a TAFE course in professional writing and editing. Many writers find their voice through short stories before attempting a novel. Through the course, she put together a collection of stories, sending them out to journals, magazines, newspapers, anyone who may potentially publish them. She faced a barrage of rejections—with just one piece being published in *Island* magazine—before she started to write her first novel.

Past the Shallows is a beautiful, moody, dark story of a family of fishermen, set on Bruny Island, south of Hobart. Favel had lived in a similar community for a short time, a place she found discomforting in a way she couldn't put her finger on as a child, but which stayed with her into adulthood. She remembered its remoteness, an abalone town with three pubs, the underlying alcoholism, the footy and violence. It wasn't lawless, but it had its own rules.

'To me,' she said in a 2011 interview with the *Sydney Morning Herald*, 'the setting became one of the main characters in the book, as it brings something dark, sad and ancient to the story.'[2] Initially, she didn't want to set her novel there, but it kept rising up in the writing until she surrendered to it.

In the *Past the Shallows*, the Curren brothers, Joe, Miles and Harry, are left in the care of their violent, alcoholic father after the death of their mother. Each of the boys has a complicated relationship with the sea—Joe and Miles find solace in surfing to escape the tough work on their father's abalone boat, while the youngest, Harry, is terrified of the ocean. Favel's passion for surfing was at its height throughout the writing of the book. It gave her the language she needed to write the boys authentically, entwining their experience of the ocean with her own—the understanding of the subtle changes in wind and tide and current, the way she would wake in the night and know it had turned offshore.

Past the Shallows was released in 2011 to critical acclaim. It sold internationally and was shortlisted for the Miles Franklin Literary Award in Australia. It won the 2012 Dobbie Literary Award for a first published work by a female author, and Favel won Newcomer of the Year at the Australian Book Industry Awards in the same year.

There are some beautiful surfing scenes in the novel, though Favel encountered the same problem other surfer/writers have— how to describe the essence of what you know so intimately to an audience, most of whom have never surfed. This led to arguments with her editor about authentic language. A small example she gives is the term 'lines backed up to the horizon'. A surfer's heart will quicken at the reference, but Favel's editor questioned whether it should read as 'swell' rather than 'lines'. But it had to be how a surfer would think, and Favel stuck to her guns. She refused to dumb it down, believing that people unfamiliar with it would come to the language of their own accord.

In music, the problems associated with the difficult second album are well known. In writing, especially after a successful first novel, the second book presents an entirely new challenge. A writer has a whole life to write their first novel but when they've established a tentative foothold in the literary world with a strong first book, the deadlines become shorter as their publisher seeks to trade on their initial success. Again, Favel went looking for the language of the water, though this time in an entirely different way. After a one-month stint on Macquarie Island, deep in the South Pacific Ocean, Favel applied for—and was awarded—an Antarctic Arts Fellowship. This got her a place on the Australian supply vessel *Aurora Australis*, and a six-week trip to Casey base in Antarctica.

This experience led to Favel falling deeply in love with the Southern Ocean. It wasn't the continent she was headed to that would captivate her, it was the mesmerising expanse of ocean she had to cross to get there that found its way into her heart and into her writing. Unlike her experience on the *Princess Of Tasmania*, she found her sea legs early on the voyage, so while the massive rolling swells they encountered would have been hell for some, she loved them—the bigger the better. She talks animatedly about the ship rising and falling through an eleven-metre swell, explaining it's not the size that matters but the space between swells. On board the *Aurora* she listened to the stories of the ship encountering eighteen-metre swells, big enough to smash porthole windows. And she slept better than she ever had, even when she had to wedge herself into her bunk to stop from falling out during the night. Eventually, she felt the swell was rolling through her as much as the ship.

Antarctica itself didn't hold Favel in the same thrall as the journey across the Southern Ocean. The continent was beautiful in a bleak way, the muted colours a million shades of white and blue. But it was a desert, with very little life on the ice, and Favel kept a watchful eye on the ship anchored just off the shelf. She couldn't wait for the return journey.

Back in the Torquay shack, into the rhythm of morning surfs and long writing days, Favel's second book, *When the Night Comes*, began to take shape. Set in the cold and grey Hobart of her childhood, *When the Night Comes* centres on a young girl, Isla, and her friendship with Bo, a cook on the Antarctica supply ship, *Nella Dan*. The *Nella Dan* was a real ship, plying the Southern Ocean from the early 1960s until she was scuttled off Macquarie Island in 1987, after running aground in a storm.

Published in 2014, *When the Night Comes* was longlisted for the Miles Franklin Literary Award and shortlisted for a number of other prestigious literary prizes. Favel is proud of these achievements, but of more importance to her were the connections she made with an entire community, mostly in Denmark, that still existed around the *Nella Dan*. When she initially reached out to former crew members, families and expeditioners, they were wary, hardly bothering to respond to the emailed questions from a young Australian writer they didn't know. But everything changed when one of the original crew, who was still working in shipping, agreed to meet her over coffee when he was in Melbourne. After that meeting, all the old crew members wanted to talk to her. She travelled to Denmark and met with as many as she could. 'This usually involved beer and food,' she says. 'I was treated like an old friend and invited into family homes. It was such an honour. We ate *smørrebrød* and fried herring with raw egg yolk, and meatballs with pickled cucumber. And, of course, there was always strong black coffee and beer. Lots of beer!'

Following the phenomenal success of *Past the Shallows*, there were huge expectations for *When the Night Comes*. Favel had established herself as one of Australia's rising literary talents and her new release was eagerly anticipated by a legion of fans. She toured extensively around the country, appearing at bookshops, libraries and festivals. Promotional tours like this are largely unpaid, designed to create momentum in the market and to sell as many books as possible. For the author, the first few events are a buzz. They finally have the opportunity to talk about this thing they've been shaping and fretting over for years. But touring is also relentless, as night after night, week after week, they are asked the same questions by different interviewers, constantly reminding themselves to sound fresh and open, as though they are hearing the question for the first time.

To see Favel in this environment is an insight into why she has endeared herself to Australia's literary community. She leans in towards the audience and they lean in to her. Her voice takes on a lilting quality as though she is letting her listeners in on a secret. She smiles easily and is quick to laugh but is also earnest when she talks about her commitment to the story she has told. She understands the unwritten contract between a writer and their readers, in particular their longing for connection. At Favel's gigs, the audience is encouraged to feel they are on first-name terms. At the signing table afterwards, people often don't just want a photo with her, they want to give her a hug.

Publicity tours are essential to selling her books but they also take Favel away from the things that sustain her—like paddling out at first light at Torquay Point, watching the sun lift itself out of the sea, chatting with the members her little community of daybreakers, and catching waves on her longboard. She's still not a summer person, preferring the crisp, cold winter mornings, the ice-cream headache of that first duck dive, the bite of the stiff north-westerly that will blow for days on end. The girl from Hobart, huddling against the cold and rain on the ferry jetty, has grown into the woman who embraces the ocean, who has found her balance in it and who, among a very select few Australian writers, has been able to translate her love of the water into stories that connect and bind us.

Jeff Raglus calls Aireys Inlet home. As an artist and musician, he was drawn to this little community on the Great Ocean Road in the mid '90s because it was everything the bigger towns like Torquay weren't. It was small, artsy and alternative—and of course there was surf. Aireys is notable for the Split Point Lighthouse that stands on the bluff overlooking the vast reach of Bass Strait. Largely destroyed in the Ash Wednesday bushfires in 1983, the town is a mix of older places that somehow survived the flames and newer houses that stretch across the Painkalac Creek and up onto the ridges of Fairhaven. For most people, Aireys is a town you pass through on the way to the more notable attractions of the Great Ocean Road—Lorne, Apollo Bay and the Twelve Apostles—but that tends to be the way the locals like it.

Though the coast around Aireys doesn't have the variety of surfing options offered by Torquay, there are a couple of quality reef breaks and a long stretch of sandy beach heading west from the Painkalac estuary. The beaches from Fairhaven to Eastern View are well positioned to catch swell, the best banks forming where hidden reefs hold the sand for long periods of time.

Like Mick, Jeff discovered the ocean early in life, though it took him a while to commit to living by it. The son of a builder, he grew up in the Melbourne suburb of Glenroy, a tough, working-class area where a boy learned to survive on his wits and by knowing how to sense violence before it erupted. Sharpie gangs ruled the streets and at various times Jeff found himself in dangerous situations, randomly punched by strangers or threatened with knives. The street life of Glenroy helped determine one thing for Jeff—as soon as practicable, he would get out of Melbourne.

Two events in 1970 shaped his life. His father built a couple of houses at Queenscliff and Point Lonsdale, small holiday towns on the coast close to Port Phillip Heads. Seeing the waves at Lonsdale Front Beach, Jeff scoured the *Trading Post* for a board he could afford and found a second-hand Okanui he liked. That same year, he moved from Glenroy Primary to the more prestigious Essendon

Grammar, where he had to learn an instrument. For no reason he can remember, he picked up a trumpet, and was able to play it 'sort of okay' within a couple of weeks. He had a trumpet and he had a surfboard, and his life would never be the same again.

True to his vow to escape Melbourne, and fresh out of school, Jeff moved to Point Lonsdale in the mid '70s and began work as a builder's labourer. In those days Lonny was known for its aggressive localism. The waves were good, especially the reef break at Glaneuse, but most surfers on the west coast avoided going there for fear of their windscreens being waxed or their tyres slashed. It took a while, but Jeff found acceptance in the line-up and, being a goofy-footer, the barrelling left at Glaneuse suited him. By his own admission, he became a complete surf bum, eventually losing his job because of his devotion to the water. He slipped easily into the counterculture that was surfing in the late '70s and was swept up in what he calls 'the do it yourself and move to the country vibe'. Magazines like *Tracks* reinforced his hippie view of the world—a side of surfing he loved but now considers lost forever.

The first band Jeff played with, the aptly named Salty Dogs, was a reggae outfit that included Rose Bygrave, who would later join Goanna and add her searing vocals to 'Solid Rock'. The Salty Dogs had regular gigs at the Ozone Hotel in Queenscliff and Jeff's trumpet suited their sound perfectly. And the gigs fitted well around his devotion to surfing. But after three years, he began to feel the isolation, both social and artistic, of the small-town life Lonny offered. And there were no girls! The Salty Dogs were headed to Melbourne and Jeff wanted to open up his life and explore where his music might take him. And that meant leaving the coastal life behind.

He found himself working as a builder's labourer again and washing bricks for his father. Steering well clear of Glenroy, he fell in love with the vibrant inner-city life offered by St Kilda and Fitzroy. Unlike the northern suburbs, they were centres of alternative arts and culture, and they allowed Jeff to immerse himself in a new life, where performing was integral rather than peripheral. As much as he missed having the surf five minutes away, he didn't miss the social isolation of Point Lonsdale.

It's a common trope that musicians, especially young and struggling ones, move through a succession of bands until something sticks and they find the one that fits—or the one where they fit. In 1985 Jeff joined the Black Sorrows, fronted by Joe Camilleri. They had been together for three years and Jeff would only stay with them for twelve months but it was the first time he earned a regular wage playing music. He also learned how hard a band had to work, how much touring they needed to do and how tight the financial side of even a successful band could be. Surviving as a musician required a strong work ethic, a lesson Jeff would carry with him for the next thirty years.

It was around this time that Jeff began designing T-shirts and band posters, experimenting with a different form of art. Again, his skills were self-taught, but his quirky designs gathered a following among bands and punters in Melbourne. He left the Black Sorrows and eventually landed in one of the seminal bands of the late '80s and early '90s, the Bachelors from Prague. The Bachelors were the epitome of inner-city cool, a fusion of new jazz and punk, and they were all about style. They wrote their own songs and had a frenetic stage show that drew a strong following among of music fans. It was also around this time that Jeff met his partner, Vicki.

The band's frontman was Henry Maas, who established the famous Black Cat café in Brunswick Street, Fitzroy. When Jeff first joined the Bachelors, his hippie surfie vibe didn't fit with Henry's dictates about the band's style. 'Great trumpet,' he said. 'But get a haircut and a decent suit.'

With his new haircut and a cheap op-shop suit, the band opened doors for Jeff to the thriving Fitzroy arts scene. Henry encouraged the Bachelors to experiment with other art forms. Jeff was still producing posters and T-shirts but now he began painting more seriously, exhibiting his work in the hotels the band played at on national tours. The association with the band gave him a ready audience for his art. His first solo exhibition was in a framing shop next door to the Black Cat, followed by a larger one at Marios, another Brunswick Street institution. Importantly for Jeff, his work began selling to people who liked it for its intrinsic value, and not just because the artist was the trumpeter in the Bachelors.

Meanwhile the band flourished, touring nationally and internationally, performing in London, Italy and at the Edinburgh Festival. Jeff started painting and designing for Mambo Graphics, giving his work even more exposure. Mambo was part of a new surf art movement, a bit left-wing, cutting-edge and rude—all of which appealed to Jeff. He worked with Mambo through most of the '90s, until the company was bought out, becoming more mainstream and, as far as Jeff was concerned, losing their edge.

Throughout this time in Melbourne Jeff continued his connection with the water, heading down to Point Lonsdale, Winki or Bells once or twice a week, often hungover and sleep deprived after gigging all night. Surfing took on a different meaning when he wasn't living on the coast with his favourite wave at his back door. He pored over the weather maps in the newspaper, looking for the tightly packed lines of deep lows in the Southern Ocean, trying to pick the best time to make a run for the coast. The sea maintained its pull on him, the need to immerse himself in salt water, to feel the power of a reef break under his feet and to enjoy the slower, less frantic qualities of life on the coast. While touring, he would often lobby to divert the bus to beaches along the way, trying to convince the band members to at least get in for a swim. Largely they ignored him, and it nagged at him, this difference. The sea was in his blood, but it was a difficult fit with the life of a working musician. Somewhere inside him, the idea of returning to live on the coast was building momentum.

As successful as the Bachelors were, Henry had a policy of everyone being on a set wage, with the rest of the money poured back into expensive video clips and extravagant live performances. By now, Jeff and Vicki had two kids and a house in Northcote with a mortgage, and the two hundred dollars a week he drew from the band wasn't enough to pay the bills. But his paintings were selling for reasonable money and the Mambo work was going well. He left the Bachelors and formed The Feeling Groovies, a band with a distinctive trancey funk sound. They put out three albums and for the first time Jeff began to make decent money out of music. He was writing his own songs and signed with Joe Camilleri's publishing company, Head Records.

Finally, in 1995, Jeff and Vicki sold their house in Melbourne and moved to Aireys Inlet. When Jeff reflects on this now, he realises there was an edge of guilt attached to the decision. Vicki needed convincing about small-town coastal life, there would be limited options for the kids once they hit secondary school and less places for Jeff to exhibit his art. He had to drive back and forth from Melbourne regularly to play gigs with The Feeling Groovies at The Night Cat, Henry Maas' club. On the positive side, the town was close-knit and they soon found their place in the community. Jeff loved the culture of Melbourne but on the coast, he could stand out a little more and his distinctive style drew attention. He started showing at Qdos Art Gallery in Lorne and formed his own band, The Beachniks.

The Beachniks are as close as Jeff has come to playing surf music. 'We don't do Dick Dale covers,' he says, 'but we do sound like a lot of coastal influences rolled into something weird and unique that sounds a bit *surf*. We call it nu-surf sound.' Similarly, when he began a long-term project performing with Vicki under the title of Victoriana Gaye, they were often told—particularly when touring in Europe—they had a distinctive surf sound. Jeff puts it down to the combination of guitar and the mariachi sound of his trumpet.

Jeff has always thought that surfing complements rather than influences both his art and music. He has managed to make a living without formal training in either. His artistic style is something even he finds hard to define. His influences vary from modernist cartoons of the 1950s and 1960s, to Picasso, Dalí and Paul Klee. Though he doesn't really paint surf images, he admits to being influenced by some of the great surf artists like John Severson and

Rick Griffin. Jeff says he is unconcerned by genres, though the term 'pop art' probably comes closest to defining his style.

Jeff now lives in a comfortable house on a dirt road close to the surf. It is one of the few houses in this part of Aireys that survived the Ash Wednesday fires. His studio sits behind the house, the windows looking out onto a native garden. On the day we meet to talk about his life as an artist and musician, he's part way through a large painting that stands on an easel in the middle of the room. He's been thinking about it during the night and has made some significant changes to it that morning. He says every day brings a new perspective. In the painting, a green sea laps at the base of mountains folding down to meet it from a pink sky. A boulder stack dominates the foreground, rising out of the sea. The cartoonish, pop art influence is obvious, but the style is more distinctive, singular. As we talk, his eyes dart to the painting as though he's memorising changes he will make later.

Jeff has the unworried face of a man comfortable in his world, with a broad forehead and greying stubble. He now alternates between three bands, all local, and exhibits his paintings regularly at galleries up and down the east coast. As successful as he has been, it hasn't been easy for him to make a living as an artist, constantly having to promote himself, set up gigs, produce art for more exhibitions and perform onstage. He attributes much of his work ethic and sense of style to his parents. In Jeff's words, his dad was a very do-it-yourself type of man. He notes that Reg Mombassa's dad was also a builder. Reg is a fellow artist, best known for his work at Mambo, and as a musician was a founding member of Mental As Anything. Jeff's mum was into interior design and her love of colour rubbed off on him.

Surfers aren't exempt from the effects of age and, at sixty, Jeff readily admits he's a different surfer now. The ocean still exerts its pull on him, but he approaches it differently. He doesn't surf big anymore. No-one likes the hold-downs and, like lots of older surfers, he doesn't feel he has to prove himself in the water. He's more easily satisfied in a session, happy to get a few waves and enjoy sitting out the back, peering at the horizon and shooting the breeze with friends. Surfing has changed enormously since the 1970s and Jeff seems happy to work his way around the less attractive aspects of it. He loathes aggression in the water and while the crowds are drawn to the big-name breaks of the west coast, he's happy to find a quieter bank and snag a couple of waves midweek. The counterculture aspect of surfing that so attracted him back at Point Lonsdale in the 1970s has all but vanished, and he mourns its passing. Now, surfing's influence on his life and art is drawn from the feeling of fitness and wellbeing he gets from being in the water. It allows him the luxury of time, a space to clear his head for a couple of hours before returning to the studio. He is known in the water and there's never a shortage of conversation. Like many ageing surfers, he struggles with the FOMO that comes with the sea-affected life, the nagging feeling that if it's offshore and the swell is up, he should be out there. An injury last year meant he wasn't able to surf for a while, but he took to swimming at a local protected beach, and loved it. It brought the realisation that if the time came when he could no longer surf, the ocean would still provide.

As an artist, a musician and a surfer, Jeff has reached a point where he is confident enough to know he doesn't have to please anyone other than himself. It's taken him sixty years to get here, but the feeling is liberating. There are no roads other than age and experience that can transport a person to this point, a place of acceptance where they are free to express themselves unburdened by the expectations of others. The life of an artist is a precarious one, subject to the whims of others, their decisions to buy a particular painting or go and see a particular band. It's a life that needs to be negotiated as much as lived, a life where balance is essential to survival. Looking at Jeff sitting in his studio, surrounded by canvases and the detritus of paint and brushes, you get the sense he's found the balance that works for him. Self-taught, self-driven, he has achieved a great deal, this Glenroy boy whose talent has taken him around the world.

The sea-affected life is one lived mindful of the smallest shift in the wind or pulse in the swell. It's the signs you look for when you get close to the coast—the windsock on top of the surf shop, the glimpse of swell through a fold in the hills, the number of cars in the carpark. It's the compulsive need to be immersed in the vastness of the ocean. And it lies at the core of the art Mick, Favel and Jeff create—wherever their talents have taken them, they have felt the pull of the ocean. Their art is not just an interpretation of what they see and feel in the water, but an expression of the sea as a constant in their lives.

Don't You Know You've Got Legs? A Gold Coast Surf Culture Manifesto
Sally Breen

The Gold Coast and surfing are synonymous, no-one would argue much against that—a connection embedded right there in the name, the Gold Coast, fifty-seven kilometres of glowing white-sand coastline rimmed along the strip with resort-style high-rises and an urban sprawl stretching back to the subtropical rainforest. With three hundred days of sunshine on average a year, the Gold Coast's list of A1 surfing-related box-ticks is long. Home to a key event on the World Surf League Championship Tour, recently renamed Corona Open, the city has produced more surfing world champions and legends than anywhere else in the country, in groundswells of brilliance, from the renegades to the 'Bronzed Aussies', to the multi-generational 'Coolie Kids' to the ambassadors. Household names that roll off the tongue: Michael Peterson, Pete Townend, Wayne 'Rabbit' Bartholomew, Mick Fanning, Joel Parkinson and seven-time world champ Stephanie Gilmore to name a few. The offices of *Surfing Life*, Australia's most iconic surfing magazine, were housed in the Old Burleigh Theatre Arcade overlooking one of the city's most prized beach breaks. Big three surfing company Billabong was born here and new-wave boutique offerings such as Rhythm are carving out a new-generation slice. In some ways, the Gold Coast Superbank, a man-made surf break pumping the longest continuous wave ride in the world from Snapper Rocks to Kirra, has driven the acceleration. You can feel it in the streets, the strange duality of being in the sixth largest city in Australia still overrun by shirtless or rashie-clad surfers, grommets, salt dogs— boards under their arms, riding bikes, running lights, gliding by on skateboards or jumping fences barefoot to get to the sea. It's there in the surf-worshipping architecture, high-rises called

Surfers Hawaiian, Bahia and The Breakers (in the old era), now super sleek towers branded Oracle, Jewel and Soul to fit the new-millennium mood—the semiotics of surfing selling everything in this city from ice-creams to real estate to beach chic homewares. But the connection between surfing and the Gold Coast writ large has not always been easy or recognised for what it is.

And it is not just because that resistance has come from external forces, the lack of cultural recognition slung around for decades about the GC like so much B-grade journalism confetti; the resistance also has a history of coming from within—not only from policymakers and officials who failed to recognise surfing's enormous economic and cultural potential but from those who have held, and in some cases continue to hold, status and power in the scene itself.

In the paragraphs that unfold here I'll attempt to unravel the intricate webs, the complex tissue of stories and codes that drive surf culture on the Gold Coast and how one cannot be read without some understanding of the other. They are of a piece. To map this story it will be necessary for me to go back, to mine my own experience, to interview players big and small, to notice the surf culture unfurling all around me with new eyes, to wonder why I got so close to surfing culture but never took it up, to see how my writing career has been infused and affected by what some people, and I, might have even referred to at some point as just a bunch of skegs. The whole process has been intimidating and maddening but most of all illuminating. The web has revealed itself.

In one of the most biodiverse regions in the world, the Gold Coast is a complex ecosystem that very rapidly turned from a genteel holiday spot for the Brisbane elite, when governor Sir Anthony Musgrave built a seaside retreat for himself and his entourage in the 1890s in Southport, to a national playground in the mid to late twentieth century, to the *Miami Vice* version of Gotham City or Vegas or wherever else, real or imagined, we see today. In the stairwell to the Surf World Gold Coast museum in Currumbin a large plaque rests as if declaring a manifesto: 'The clique became a cult and the cult became a culture.' The same could be said of the city.

When I lived in Mermaid Beach in the mid 2000s, the local council erected a near six-foot steel fence straight down the middle of the Gold Coast Highway running the length of the strip dividing the suburban sprawl from the coveted beachside. It was designed to be very difficult to jump, at an awkward height, the skinny median strip running perilously close to cars, the whole feat even harder with a board. The council wanted us all to cross at the lights. It was about our safety, they said, the four-lane highway, a Frogger game for surfers, skaters and beachgoers scurrying over the asphalt, towels billowing like capes. Hitting the water was the goal, as fast as possible. Every night some sea-salt Robin Hood with a boltcutter would snap a big hole in that fence, sometimes leaving part of it swinging in the wind narrowly missing traffic. The council workers would remount that section of fence, solder heavier clips and the next day the hole would appear somewhere else. The war went on. For months. And we were grateful. But then it stopped—perhaps Robin moved away—more likely he was undone by ramped-up CCTV.

For me, the connection between surf culture and the city I call home is something more than just a perfect storm of environment, critical mass and means, the linkage that erupts when you have a big city highway and a string of lit beaches running parallel—it's symbiotic. Symbiosis, by definition, meaning the interaction between two different organisms living in close physical association, typically to the advantage of both. If we think of this city as an organism and its surf culture as one too, we can see their stories have developed in tandem, they've grown up together, mirrored each other, fed on and bolstered each other's unfurling. The Viennese writer Hermann Broch once claimed that, 'Those who live by the sea can hardly form a single thought of which the sea would not be part.' Surfing runs a line through our lives here, direct, indirect, subliminal; there are points of convergence everywhere, ways that won't leave you alone even when you want them to, infused, ground in—that's how it is when you live here. The tide of these things washes over us. But I didn't always think this way.

Surfing the Grunge Soup—GC Surf Culture in the 1990s

I arrived on the Gold Coast at the tail end of a blisteringly hot January 1992. I was here to study at the freshly minted Gold Coast campus of Griffith University—in a city of perpetually new things. The degree, a Bachelor of Arts in Creative Arts, was the first of its kind in Australia—a mash-up of creative writing, visuals arts and theatre, less like *Fame* and something more like the art school version of the Gravitron—where we bit off more than we could chew and held on for dear life; a ragtag bag of arty kids come from all over, bunnies to the experiment. We'd had to audition to get in and thought that made us special. Looking back, I guess it kinda did. We pooled into cheap share houses in Labrador and Southport in our Doc Martens and black jeans, wasting no time getting high and complaining about the heat. We burrowed into these microscopic worlds in the burbs as if the rest of the city wasn't out there, sliding between the campus and other people's houses and shitty flats in a tornado of art student fumes and bias. We coveted gothic candelabras. Good grades. Each other. Experimental noise projects in front rooms happened way more than visits to the beach—which seemed to only ever happen at night, in the dark, when someone with a car could drive you there and your eyes were pinging. My skin was so white it was ghostly. The city was a supersonic wasteland of fun in the sun, so, we avoided it mostly. Or tried to. The thing was, like strands of seaweed unspooling in rivulets, the ocean and the city, in all its fairyland wonder, began creeping into the poems and stories we were writing, the art we were making, into our dreams.

If I'm honest, no matter how punk I ever tried to get, the sea was always there, rolling around inside me. It had been there since my fat baby-face first felt the salty scratch of a towel on a Sydney beach. My mum, a ten-pound Pom who'd bake until she was golden, and my dad, a Manly lifesaver who loved to swim out past the breakers. By the time my brother came along my father had taken up a transfer to Brisbane, but the water never really left us. Creeks, storms, suburban pools, that was just what a South East Queensland life was: finding water and getting inside it. Weekend runs to Bribie Island or the Sunshine Coast, sometimes holidays on the GC in buildings called Seacrest or Pacific Point or the Chateau, our dad launching us onto waves as if we were pliable kid-sized dolphins. Long summer stints in Forster, New South Wales, with bronzed cousins and their entourages on One Mile Beach, where the back door of my aunty and uncle's house hit the soft shaded sand of the beach track, always cool on the toes, as if it was still holding the night inside it. If we weren't flying out the front of waves on our boogie boards, my bro and I spent a lot of our time with our feet moving around in the fishy slosh at the bottom of boats.

Once I left school, and the panopticon of the parental eye, I tunnelled further and further away from the sea. Not literally, I could have gotten myself on a beach within an hour or so, but in a parallel universe kind of way. The tunnels I scurried down all related to the night, dark alleyways, shaded rooms, hidden theatres, basement-level recording studios. The arts and music scene in Brisbane was mushrooming and I was Alice, mooching around the underground, dying my naturally blonde tresses black. I wasn't thinking about the ocean. But the sea waits: once it gets inside you, the sea always wants you back.

My life ran smack up against surfing culture again in my second year of university when the novelty of the life hadn't worn off exactly but had gotten scratchy. The share houses collapsing under our rapidly developing capacity for high drama and in some cases, the creeping grip of heroin. I'd already seen where that road led to in Brisbane—nowhere good—so I bounced out and moved in with the nerdiest girl in our year, closer to the Broadwater in Labrador. The move worked: my grades went from middling to straight A's but I was broke and bored. I needed a job. And I got one—working for one of the biggest surfing retail franchises in the region, City Beach. My neighbour had pulled some strings. I didn't surf, and I didn't look the part, but I guess I looked okay enough to pass—my manager seemed impressed I could write a sentence and I helped her compose her missives to head office. From the first day I stepped into that shop in the Dolphin Arcade in Surfers Paradise, it was as if I'd let out breath. The shop itself was overstocked, a surf brand money machine and mostly boring. It was the people who worked there that intrigued me. Older than the sixteen-year-olds the owners packed the Pacific Fair store with, this crew were in their early to mid twenties, surfers and skaters who walked the walk and looked like a GC version of a Californian dream. The girls, megawatt: bright eyes, exposed midriffs—all long hair, platform sneakers, health. I couldn't talk to them about Lacan and that was part of the attraction. And the boys, ultra-cool, so laidback they were always staring off into space as if dreaming of something they'd never tell you about. Uniform of knee-length quick-dries, boxy surf and band shirts, skate shoes—Etnies, Globes, DCs—bright white socks to mid-calf, Arnette sunglasses, chunky silver chains running from their belts to their pockets.

Maybe fantasising about each other in that surf shop was inevitable, the long hours stuck in a cheap wood-panelled tomb, with the same surf videos playing on high rotation and the stereo wars erupting when we all got sick of watching big wave dominations over and over, and selling bag after bag of Quiksilver T-shirts to Chinese tourists. The war usually went: me and all the guys playing punk, Unwritten Law, Deftones, NOFX versus all the girls playing 'Barbie Girl' by Aqua—and who wouldn't want to party when you looked like that? We'd close out shifts at The Rose & Crown, a sticky glorious shithole that catered to broad cross-section of misfits, basically anyone who couldn't stand the Cocktails and Dreams–style clubs on Orchid Avenue, and one of the few places in the strip where you could hear live bands. A scene ripe for the picking.

The Rose & Crown

(*Writing a poem by asking people in the Rosie what
their three favourite things in the world are and writing
it down on beer coasters*)

beer, girl, money
Canada, horses, dogs
lights, blue, green
sex, drugs, girls

money, fun, happiness
sharing my dreams and helping other people get there,
    spreading good karma

women, money, beach
you, travelling, surfing
life, girlfriend, pot
drinking, drugs, women
dog, surfboard, sex

asparagus sandwiches, lesbians and Aussie Rules

rum, big cars, big waves
surfing, rum, sex
rum, pot, friends
chocolate, sex, friends
friends, family, sex

a tip truck full of beer, a tip truck full of money and a
lifetime full of happiness

alcohol, sex, music
alcohol, g-strings, cleavage
alcohol, drugs, girls
alcohol, football, sex

alcohol, music, females and surfing in the morning
(can I have four?)

my car, money and I dunno gee that's hard
my car, my mum and other people's money

my son, sex and beautiful clothes
my son, drugs and manly hot bodies
my son, country music and my 1979 fender telecaster

e, surf, sex
mull, speed, e
sex, you, the rosie
her, beer, the rosie

sex, travelling, boys
cocksucking cowboys, Bacardi lemon and lime,
vodka, lime and soda

surfing, sex, chilling
career, stability, travelling
music, generational diversity and that's it
chocolate, Matchbox 20 and Brad Pitt

girlfriend, surfing, making money
boyfriend, mull, good times
alcohol, motorbikes and living in the bush without a
     hassle in the world

The ocean, the air in my lungs and the Vatican
     (you know, where the Pope lives)

That's the thing about this world, it was predictable on so many levels until it wasn't. The booze, babes and bulbs mentality shot through with an electric line of wit, eccentricity, gen X culture. A dropout slacker philosophy that had morphed into an off-the-grid, non-conformist ideal, keeping it real and pure or mad and sick—and a lot of that vibe led back to surfing.

I went to the bars and the parties, but I didn't go bake on the beach. I still had to write and study when my lifestyle diversions allowed it. I moved to Main Beach where the crew from the shop and their people hung out (I'd never live further than the Southport bridge—they'd tell me, eyes bulging—as if living away from a beach break was akin to the end of the world). I settled in and the surf scene was a tonic, got me through all the deconstruction, the intense competitiveness of my peers, the pressure of trying to be someone better than I was. I needed somewhere chill to escape to and three beers deep in a house full of surfers and skaters was never a bad place to be.

Waves of Mutilation—Boys, Bongs and the End of an Era

Back then, Main Beach was different: you could still smell the money, the perfumed waft of the white-shoe brigade, but there was also run-off, detritus, flotsam and jetsam and enough crumbling old beach shacks, cheapish apartments and two-storey walk-ups to house us—the beach houses set back from the road, on giant blocks, rats scurrying in the sandy soil under wind-bitten decks. Tedder Avenue was pumping—during the day it was stacked with shirtless surfers, shocks of sun-bleached hair and sixpacks gleaming like rows of oversized toasted hazelnuts, pooling outside the infamous local bakery, wolfing down vanilla slices and jam donuts. It was always hard to get a seat. When a Goldsteins franchise appeared across the road, the well-heeled tended to go there instead, maybe it was for the comfort of the branding that went better with their pastel-coloured Polo Ralph Lauren shirts; more likely it was to avoid, as best they could, the rowdy banter of the unfiltered directly opposite. At night, bars like Blu Grotto catered to the rising techno tide and a rollcall of hot young women with tabs of e shoved into their fuck-me boots while the old guard faded into their chardonnays on the al fresco tables in the better restaurants. At night the worlds often merged—especially in the long dark alleyway running behind the restaurants and bars where all the action was, apprentice chefs smoking and selling next to the empty kegs, suited entrepreneurs ranting into their mobile phones, girls trying to sneak their way into something for free, until the pavements got wobbly, the fairy lights in the palm trees blurry, and you found yourself in the high-rise apartment of a Gold Coast entrepreneur i.e. con man drinking his top-shelf scotch trying to avoid his clutches or a middle-aged camp dude decked out in Versace who'd once done interior decoration for

Elton John—his apartment taking up a whole floor of a high-rise replete with mosaic mirrored walls and life-size ceramic black panthers. The rich might have had all the cash—but we looked good.

Today Main Beach glistens like a shiny superyacht with no-one on it. Impressive, but eerily quiet as if it's forgotten about the fuller throttle speed it was made for. Polished new-edition Mercedes-Benzes and Porsche SUVs gliding into gated grounds, fortress towers, where no-one ever appears on the balconies, as if the people inside are too brittle and fragile for actual wind. The only houses left are *Vogue Living* sprawls with imposing garage doors and security cameras swivelling. Driving along Tedder Avenue, it's as if everyone has died or is about to. The well-coiffed couples alighting gingerly from the soft-close doors of their chariots to buy gourmet dog food for their chihuahuas and shih tzus have priced their suburb out of a personality. The median rent price three times the minimum wage and the shops along the avenue closing at a rate of knots. A foreshadowing of the kind of real estate squeeze that's slowly making its way down the coast, through all the other beachside precincts, a relentless development push, the pursuit of what the CSIRO has called the Gold Coast's 'path dependence',[1] a track set in the Wild West development era of the '50s through to the '80s, when standard development practices were ignored by a renegade council and everything got rubberstamped. A place where the continued levelling of 'old' structures does more than usher in the latest shiniest aesthetic, it effectively eliminates the presence of the working class.

It's hard to believe Mainy was once cool, with one of the best video stores on the coast. The tiny flat I lived in at the front end of a two-storey walk-up on Breaker Street is miraculously still there, one of the last remaining, flanked on either side by houses with surfaces that never corrode or die. That little set of rooms where I once woke to a stranger sitting on my couch at one am tripping off his head. The place where I rewrote my honours thesis on a fridge-sized PC so one of my surf shop colleagues didn't get divorced because of all the stories I'd written about her, even though she did anyway, the pad where an old uni friend arrived one night to try to beat me up, and where the Indy 500 used to rip through the streets—corralling us in a lockdown storm of petrol and parties. Tripping between one beach shack and the next was kind of a Main Beach thing, treats in hand. Sublime, the musical weapon of choice—a Californian ska punk outfit who seemed to embody the mood of the times, their tunes a mash-up of Cali-Caribbean nights, dirty boulevards and bad tattoos rolling out of every house and low-rise apartment block. 'Got to find a reason, reason things went wrong/got to find a reason why my money's all gone.'[2] The journey between the houses often more adventurous than the reality where I'd tend to get bored in five minutes, with all the boys going on, like boys tend to do.

To amuse myself I developed a series of lo-fi crushes on a Bermuda Triangle of said boys. There was Jake, an American surfer whose impenetrability and detachment hung around him like a layer of very sexy ozone; Mark, a punk skater with enough chain, nose ring and Billy Idol hair to scare old ladies; and Wraith, the ringleader of the druggiest, funniest house beachside of anywhere, peopled with Wraith's army, a just-graduated gaggle of grommets, their puppies-in-a-bag energy infectious. Wraith was a surfer and a bodybuilder whose width seemed designed to make up for the fact that he was no Valentino. He made all the girls laugh mostly because they wouldn't sleep with him. But I liked him, sneaking into his house late at night, stepping over passed-out blondies, to his room which was off limits to everyone, apparently.

Mark was more like a buddy where the crush is best left unrequited, we rolled around once and then thought better of it. I'd trail around him in the streets after our shifts watching him ollie and grind on anything with an edge, laughing at his antics. Mark was in love with Alyssa anyway, a statuesque peroxided warrior who wore tartan skirts and steel caps. When she walked towards me everything seemed to slow down, my body going into flight mode, but she was actually very sweet.

Jake was another story. Hanging around with him in the back end of the surf shop while he punched anti-theft tags into mountains of stock does not sound like the most romantic of bonding sessions but somehow it was—Jake always made you feel as if you were in a much sadder version of a John Hughes movie, sunglasses-at-night vibe, lots of long meaningful pauses. I don't know, maybe it was the accent. I remember bittersweet times after late-night calls, lying awake in his bed. He was going back to California, nothing ever got started or had a chance to, or maybe I was reading too much into it like they all said—as poets tend to do.

The vibe in surfing at the time was hyper-masculine—or at least that's how it seemed to me. Boys who were so pumped up and self-assured on the videos and in the cheeky banter thrown around at parties, but tended to unravel or startle easily—at least for a few moments. There was so much bravado, and inside that, a community, but as my time spent among them all stretched out, a strong whiff of same same washed over everything. Rampant self-medication, perhaps even desperation. It was partly the times. I wondered about those boys. How many of them had thought about throwing themselves off of high-rises or into the sea and never coming out? It was a feverish scene and we were all in it. My uni friends mostly didn't understand me 'slumming it' as they put it and I kept the two worlds separate but there was something sad about Jake and there was something sad about Wraith. I never realised part of that sadness might have been about me. I was a chameleon changing my colours to suit the different trees.

In May 1996 Sublime frontman Bradley Nowell OD'd in a San Francisco hotel room and maybe we should have taken it as an omen.

Like all worlds that get appropriated and sold, the scenes on the televisions and in the magazines were not quite representative of what it was. I've been in other big game worlds where it felt the same. Different sport codes, the music industry. There was always a big gap between the rider and the reality. But big game and big talk sells merch and when there's money to be made no-one wants to talk about the pressures that go with competition outside the norm, a bit of ribbing and one-upmanship par for the course. No-one wants to talk about the kickback from the lifestyle, not when the lifestyle can be shot in the right light. At least they didn't back then.-

When I asked surf writer and previous *Tracks* editor Tim Baker whether they had ever run any articles on substance abuse or depression, and he said, 'Not that I can recall', I found that strange on one level and predictable on another. The remit of *Tracks* wasn't about analysis—it was all about big wave panoramas and a blokey, conversational vibe that celebrated surfing and fought in some ways against its denigration. But still. This was exactly the time when a whole generation of surfers on the Gold Coast got dragged across the reefs of a scene and left out there. Alone. There was no magic jetski to come to scoop them up. A see no evil, hear no evil state of affairs that had been lingering for a while.

In 2019 surfing legend Mark 'Occy' Occhilupo opened up about his struggles with depression and substance abuse when he was at his peak in the 1980s:

> Back then, mental health wasn't talked about. You kind of felt like whatever you were experiencing was only happening to you. There weren't really any ways to talk to other people … it was kind of weak to be going through something like that. You didn't talk about it. You tried to keep a handle on it yourself.[3]

Occy clawed his way out, reigniting his drive and channelling the traits of his addictive personality into a remarkable comeback that would see him place second to Kelly Slater in 1997 and take out the world title in 1999. But others weren't so lucky. Tim told me, 'The write-off mentality in Australian surfing was in full flight in the '80s and '90s and a full generation of Gold Coast surfers failed to live up to their potential.' Guys that could have been contenders invisible in the thirty-year gap between Rabbit winning the first world title in '78 and Mick Fanning in 2007. They all lounge around in there nursing their penalty bongs. 'Mick, Joel and Dean saw the casualties,' he told me, 'and were determined to chase their dreams.'

Just a Girl—Surfing Culture, Invisible Women and the Quest to Be Seen and Heard

Twenty-odd years later I'm teaching creative writing at the university which sprouted me, and have been in different stints since I graduated. Watching the campus grow from a four-building corral with a pop-up cafeteria in a classroom serving cans of cheap soft drink and lukewarm sausage rolls into a mini city so big it now has its own postcode. The students have come in waves too, the internationals mostly from colder places—Norway, Sweden, Canada—drawn in by heat-seeking romance, the drone shots of a city rimmed in sunshine and water that the university blasts all over its overseas advertising and digital signatures. When I first started teaching, the local kids would rock up to tutes with twenty minutes of the class to go, wet hair, unmistakable post-session glow—shoulders loose, sun soaked, taking their seat like everything was right with the world, until I'd raise an eyebrow and they'd say, 'Sorry I'm late miss,' and I'd counter, 'Surf must be good today—and don't call me miss.' They'd shrug and go red maybe, but the grin would say all I needed to know.

One of the worst offenders was Zita. An edgy young woman from outback Queensland who'd landed on the coast and taken up surfing with the same kind of attitude she did everything—full tilt. Keeping control of a class was always difficult when Zita was around. She didn't look like a GC girl. Body taut and wiry from a mix of surfing and recreationals, her clothes were more rockstar than Roxy and her platinum hair, short at the back and rising in a rockabilly-style quiff up top, meant she looked as if she's just stepped off the set of a No Doubt film clip. She was also whip smart but her ADHD tendencies and her dependency on nicotine and weed meant she was always heading outside for a hit. Small clumps of boys would follow on the pretence of needing to go to the toilet, answer a call from work, whatever. Often, I'd join them after class declining the toke and trying to connect to Zita—to get her to focus. I knew she was one of the best writers I had, but the task proved difficult. There were layers to Zita I hadn't fully cottoned onto yet, a traumatic family history and a taste for the unruly, so I'd just sit there answering her looping questions as best I could, enjoying basking in her energy, her intelligence, her command, watching the boys preening about like peacocks trying to get her attention. It never worked.

Zita tunnelled much further into the rabbit holes of the Gold Coast surfing scene than I did. After she graduated, I didn't see her for a while, maybe the occasional phone call, always funny, but underneath, this low-level hum line of static, as if she might need rescuing. Zita lived on what locals call the south coast of the Goldy, the surf scene playing out all down the strip but peaking at prized points, from those who surf South Straddy in the north to those who hang on the long stretch of coast running from Currumbin to Kirra and Coolangatta on the New South Wales border in the south. I'd heard she was running in a few different circles and that she'd struck up a friendship with a big personality in the scene. I remember once she'd just gotten back from the Bells contest at Torquay full of stories of all the crazy shit that went down—she never seemed that impressed with the boys or the groupies who congealed around them and that's probably why she was in. Zita wasn't a girl that got a backstage pass when the party was swinging, she was surfing and getting high and staying in the houses. The free rein must have been seductive.

The curious thing about this story is that when it comes to Zita's interactions, I can't name names and that says something about how the hierarchies of this local scene work. We spend over two hours talking online about her surfing life and a big chunk of it remains off the record. Zita knows things. She's seen what it's like to be considered one of the boys, and what it feels like when you're not, always stuck somewhere in between, she wasn't pro, she wasn't lineage, she was scrapping for everything she ever learned. And always this idea that maybe if she was magically good enough it would prove her own self-worth, she'd be accepted, the gates would open up to a kind of mythical surfing nirvana that was actually all in her head.

Zita conveys the story to me cleanly. The guy she'd been hanging out with had become known as a wasteoid; his name, whenever I mention it to other players, is met with rolls of the eyes, dismissiveness, even though he'd apparently been troubled but brilliant. I'd felt the kickback too, in a peripheral way. How some people generate unease in a community because they rock the boat when there are reputations to protect and money to be made. Zita liked this guy because he was what you might call an outsider-insider, someone she could relate to. She soon learned that aligning yourself or considering yourself a friend might be met with resistance.

'The first time I realised very clearly there was a social code, hierarchy and standard that I would never measure up to in the very inner circles of surfing on the Gold Coast was when I happened to pass the wife of a well-known professional surfer, who I knew through social circles. I said hello and I innocently suggested, "Oh we should go walking since you live down the road, there's some good hills around here."

'I remember the look on her face. Indignant, disgusted, as if I'd stepped on the Queen's corgi or flashed a penis from a trench coat. She replied curtly, her words cooling the air, "No, I don't think so, I don't have time." To me that was a clear tipping point, when a number of other experiences had culminated in an intuitive understanding. The Gold Coast had spawned a currency system that I clearly was not able to offer anything to. I was not beautiful enough in the sense that I was I able to be coveted, I had no status, I had no partner with status or money, I was just your normal run-of-the-mill girl with no other will or energy to feign otherwise, my youth, along with my naivety, having passed a few summers before. Nor was I young enough to be exploited for anything. I was not even afforded congeniality or a sign of respect. I was dirt.'

Zita tells me she had been operating under the illusion she was part of a community, but status overran everything, status was all-important.

Zita spends a lot of time with her father now, but it wasn't always like that. Zita's family lineage is fraught with trauma and abuse, so many members of her family on both sides failed by systems and institutions, and the ricochet effects of their suffering leaked through generations. I often picture Zita's early life as some kind of kid version of *Wake in Fright*. I see her on the balcony of an outback pub in Queensland where something very real and very fucking raw is about to happen. She was a kid on the edge. And there were so many people in the local community here on the edge too. Surfing in that sense wasn't necessarily a panacea.

Zita got very sick. She told me at one stage when she hit rock bottom, she had hardly any movement left, her body was on fire. She healed herself with bone broths, integrative medicine, trauma therapy, surfing. Crucially, her relationship with the ocean had shifted from a scene-based interaction into a more embodied, essential experience. She'd had to adjust her thinking and it's a mode of engagement a lot of surfers I interviewed for this story have. The will to be better, but not necessarily to do that in view of others or a camera. To get better and excel for yourself. Surfing is a sport where you can graduate on your own terms. The thing is, Zita had felt much more pressure as a woman to belong—to be accepted, to have felicity out there, and in the end that desire had partly resulted in her not being able to move her limbs at all.

When I arrive at her townhouse in Kingscliff maybe circa 2005, I've got two bottles of wine in hand, but I'll only need one, because, well, I'm hanging out with Zita. She's slow-cooking us some lamb and tells me about her journey, trying to figure out what has been wrong with her when no doctor could. What I distinctly remember about this night is Zita raving on to me at some point about surfing magazines, how they exemplify something fucked about surfing culture she hasn't been able express or penetrate despite all her experience and education. She shows me a series of very hot shots of a young Stephanie Gilmore not surfing but posing in her bedroom in black and white, in her underpants. Stephanie has since, rightly, pushed back on this type of objectification, but for someone into sport like I was, I found the images highly sexualised in a way that was uncomfortable—from the photos you can't even recognise what kind of sport she does. Not that surprising in surfing maybe but weird as a woman operating in the twenty-first century. Why did it take so long for the surfing world to catch up? Why were women shot in these ways and so removed from their obvious ability? Why was it so threatening? This was before #MeToo, before the NRL and AFL codes finally recognised the groundswell in women's participation, before prize money in most codes was on parity. As women, this was our reality.

It reminded me of the days in the surf shop when I'd flip through the pages of those magazines on the counter and random people's coffee tables feeling uninspired and unimpressed. I was used to doing this—a detached default mechanism is often necessary as a woman, when nothing in the pages connects you to the content. It wasn't just because I couldn't necessarily read the aesthetics of a good set or the particulars of some guy busting a good air, it was because I couldn't see myself there. I wasn't there. There weren't any women present.

More recently I picked up an edition of *Tracks* thinking surely in twenty-odd years there'd been some progression. I go through it cover to cover. There are no articles on women surfers. There are no articles written by women. The only picture of a woman in the whole magazine is in an advertisement for wetsuits designed to appeal to those with a rising environmental consciousness. You can't see her face. It is what Zita would call a money shot, board under her arm in a high-cut rashy, the shot emphasising not her surfing ability or even her face, but her pert arse.

I remember some of the guys in the surf shop would rib me about why I didn't surf, trying to teach me how to ride a skateboard in the wide bowels of the arcade when it was quiet. I'd tell them, 'Jesus, man, get off my case, I bodysurf, I boogie board.'

And they'd say, 'Why? Don't you know you've got legs?'

The comment didn't sting so much as make me wonder myself. Why hadn't I stood up?

There had been pioneering women in surfing from the Gold Coast or who have lived here—Phyllis O'Donnell, Wendy Botha— but I didn't know about them then. None of the guys I'd interviewed for this story thought the marginalisation of women in surfing was a real and deliberate thing, more a consequence of larger factors, but I guess that's the difference between observing women and being one.

Gangster's Paradise—Views from the Inside

I'm standing behind the counter of my local BWS, notebook resting on a stack of shopping bags on the top of a stand with all the implements one might need to get stuck right into a bottle of booze hanging off it, shot measures, corkscrews, bottle openers and stoppers, cocktail shakers, plastic cups, party hats. I'm not working here but the rollcall of characters filing into the shop think I am—asking how's business and depending on how gone they already are, sharing mini life stories, slurred commentaries to which Mike, the real bottle-shop guy, and I feign various levels of interest. I'm here to interview him and as he bags up stock and deals with French backpackers who want bottles of Mateus, and wired locals who want the cheapest cigarettes, he tells me about his surfing life. Bottle shops in Australia have been declared an essential service in the first wave of Corona, but the going's pretty slow, so we're able to talk freely.

We start with the shark attack because, well, Jesus. He says, 'Remember when that guy nearly got taken by a shark at Lennox Head in twenty fifteen?' I nod recalling a wave of attacks around that time, all on the stretch of coast from Byron Bay through to Ballina and Lennox. Sadly, some of them were fatal. Mike says, 'Yeah, that was me.'

Mike was on his annual family holiday in Lennox about an hour and a half south of the Gold Coast on the northern New

South Wales coast. He was out surfing with his brother, it was the day after a young guy had been taken at North Wall in Ballina. There was media everywhere and they were all a bit paranoid about going out, so they went in a little later than usual, and when Mike pulled away from the main group the shark launched.

'All of a sudden it was as if my surfboard hit a rock or something.' He smashes his hands together to try to mimic the impact. 'So, my board's gone from a fairly flat position to a fairly vertical position. The shark's come along and grabbed the back of the surfboard and given it a bit of a shake. I've flopped into the water and all I recall is grabbing my board as quick as possible and luckily a wave came along and smashed into me, I smashed into somebody else trying to get out of the water.' He laughs when he says this, but I can tell how mad the scramble must have been. The very real panic of it is still in his eyes, in his muscle memory. Mike got to the beach. He tells me he just sat there for a second in shock. There were big holes in his board and the shark had eaten one fin and he remembers turning his surfboard over because he didn't want people to see. When I ask him why, he says he didn't want the attention, didn't want the media all over him, but they came anyway.

'My brother was still in the water and I thought, Gee I better get him out of there,' and we laugh at this like the delayed reaction is justified, normal. 'Anyway in the time it took me to get from the point to our holiday house, a distance of a few hundred metres, the media swarmed on us, someone had called it in … and my brother was pushing the media into me if you like, and you know, I wasn't into it at all. I'd just had this horrendous experience; I didn't need more horrendous experiences like going on national television.'

This is just the type of self-effacing guy Mike is. In all my interactions with him, some of them definitely more inebriated than others, he's what you'd call a true gentleman. We now greet each other like long-lost friends every time I enter the shop, it's kind of our thing and my mates are always amused by this—that the crew from the bottle shop are friends with me and come to my new year's parties. But the local scene in Surfers Paradise, one of the country's most frequented tourism hot spots, is like this: in a city which can be overrun by over eighty thousand visitors a day, local price and local rules are a thing.

When I ask Mike who his favourite local surfer is, he doesn't hesitate. 'I'd have to say Mick would be a favourite—more his personality than anything. I met him in Bali once, we were out in the surf, we were at this secret spot, it was him and Mason Ho and they were shooting for Red Bull, we're in the water and there are only three or four of us there and the camera crew. And I mentioned the shark attack thing, his happened about two weeks after mine and we were in the same article in *LiQUiFY*. We had a little personal moment if you like because we'd had that same experience. He's always worried about something coming from behind him and I'm always looking at the shadows. It took me a couple of weeks to get back in the water and when I did get back in, I used to hallucinate sharks and that lasted for quite a while.'

Mike's written a list of other things he wants to talk to me about on the back of a receipt. I can't read his writing all that well, but I can see one item, the difference between the old scene and the new scene and next to that in brackets is one word—pot.

'Kelly Slater was the great game changer. Back in the old days we had people like Michael Peterson with mental issues who used to use illicit drugs to self-medicate. And those people unwittingly influenced a lot of other young surfers.' Mike tells me stories about surf trips in Sri Lanka and Sumatra when he was young, with groups of guys he'd 'trapped himself with' who'd get so blazed they'd miss out on the best surf in the morning. He said Kelly Slater changed it for everyone, he'd had a dad who was an alcoholic and was openly against drugs and drinking. Mike says Kelly gave him an out. 'I wasn't really into drugs, I'm just in for the surfing, and if Kelly could say no anyone could.'

A lot has changed on the Gold Coast in that same stretch of time too. When I tell people I live in Surfers Paradise they tend to look at me as if as an alien life force has kidnapped me and forced me to do it. 'What about the bikies?' they ask. 'What about all the schoolies?' In the twenty-odd years I have lived on the Gold Coast I have never met a bikie. The only gangsters I've met have been government officials, businessmen and low-grade drug dealers who wish they were gangsters but who are actually just foot soldiers for syndicates that operate underground everywhere, not just here. When it comes to Schoolies, I've never had any overt moral panics about the sorties of rebellious youth. In fact, when they descend in their tens of thousands into my suburb for two weeks every year, I kinda like it, the high-rises turning into rampant spectacles of noise, colour and light, white curtains billowing out of open doors as if all the buildings are going to take off and fly, all the kids corralled in a giant cage on the beach, dancing around in the sand and the lasers they train all over them and out across the sea, having the kind of fun most of us have forgotten how to. It's as if everyone has erased the idea of why all these buildings are here in the first place, why the majority of schoolies continue to come here even though dribs and drabs of them might take off to Byron or Port Douglas or Bali. It's because of the unique big-city, big-ocean mix of experiences this place offers. Protecting the symbiotic strength of that mix though is going to be the problem.

In promotional footage of the Gold Coast, the city appears to explode out of the sand and its intricate man-made canal systems in a heady, high-density fusion of development, beach and water that defies logic. And in fact, it does:

> Looking at Chicago's gold coast, Spain's Costa del Sol, Mexico's Baja peninsula and Florida's Fort Lauderdale, we can see a type of urban development that is irrevocably dependent upon exploitation of waterside natural environments for hedonistic pleasure, tourism, land and property development, and conspicuous consumption. Particular environmental imaginaries have made such places 'golden' in the eyes of their developers, visitors and residents. The environmental problems facing these and other 'gold coasts' stem

from similar historical patterns of urban development, which have concentrated wealth in risky places (prone to earthquakes, tsunamis, hurricanes, flooding and/or landslides) and failed to recognise the value of local ecosystems. Urban environmental histories of gold coasts can illuminate how these places interact with the ecological processes that have shaped them.[4]

It's hard to believe but the GC 'once faced south not east and was situated near the current position of Antarctica ... Hundreds of millions of years ago it lay at the bottom of an abyssal trench, off the coast of the supercontinent Gondwana.'[5] The idea of the Gold Coast starting off as a stretch of land languishing at the bottom of an abyss lends itself to classic jokes, images of a whole bunch of meter-maid mermaids squirming around down there just waiting for their chance. The city has never lacked detractors. All the shade thrown has done zip to dent its unremitting status as the fastest-growing city in the country for over twenty years, the number-one holiday destination for domestic tourists and top five for internationals. All this unrelenting growth, though, comes at a price.

In 2013 the Gold Coast City Council spent twenty thousand dollars a day of taxpayer money on foreshore protection and beach restoration after a particularly bad season of erosion—i.e. protecting multimillion-dollar properties from falling into the sea. 'As a result of coastal development on the Gold Coast very little functioning foredune habitat remains with the exception of the Southport Spit and South Stradbroke Island.'[6] And where does controversial Gold Coast Mayor Tom Tate want to build his giant cruise ship terminal and enact his latest public land grab? The Southport Spit. A perfect storm is brewing. Tuned to a fever pitch, a war is erupting between volunteer organisation Save Our Spit, the officials elected in one of the safest liberal seats in the country and a Labor state government that appears, for the moment, to be on the side of SOS and the activist surfers and locals like Mike, who are heavily involved in it and who've lived here long enough to recognise the precarious beauty of an environment we're potentially about to lose.

There is no doubt the Gold Coast was built on the income and flow-on effects of natural resource depletion, particularly sand mining and forestry. Black gold in the form of rutile and zircon used to make ammunitions when wartime demand was high, and red gold in the form of cedar which drove the burgeoning economies of many coastal cities in this state. But how long can this disconnect between the economy and the environment continue? Early twentieth century images of the Gold Coast show a foredune landscape completely flattened by sand mining—a process favoured by government because it paved the way, literally, for development. It is in some respects the reason why we're all here.

I live in one of those high-rises that rose out of the sand in Surfers Paradise, not a shiny new one but an older-style place. The unbroken view of the Pacific Ocean it offers running from Main Beach to Coolangatta on a clear day is breathtaking. The sun rising off the horizon each morning like a supernova of neon orange nuclear fallout means I spend most of my time walking around my pad with my sunglasses on. As the years have gone by, I've learned to read this panorama in a multitude of ways—from up high, with my toes in the sand or my body in the waves—and it has infused the way I write and see. You become attuned to tidal shifts, wind variations, dangerous rips, when the breaching of a humpback whale is going to make you spill your breakfast, what times of day the rainbow lorikeets will arrive on your balcony in a chaos of colour and carnage and when the currawongs will signal the loneliness of a long night. Mostly, I've learned of all the different ways the ocean speaks. From calm and benevolent to full of untempered ferocity.

It's a vista I particularly enjoy after two am, when I'm up late writing and the rickshaws pumping Justin Bieber or Tones and I have slowed down, when the Lamborghinis and the Harley-Davidsons have stopped doing laps, when all the party people are locked down in the clubs or the bowels of the casino and the pissed bogans wandering the streets have gone back to their package-deal apartments. I live on the only stretch of beach in the city lit up 24/7 by huge banks of full-voltage floodlights. Usually a beach at night is a deep dark place flecked only by a full moon or distant shore lights catching rolling lips of whitewash, but Surfers Paradise beach is dark only at the north and south edges where the floodlights no longer reach. Out the front of my place the Esplanade glows, and the glow stretches from the sand into the sea. The thousands of seagulls that populate this area don't seem to mind, in fact they appear to prefer it, the lights drawing food sources out of the sand or attracting them into the sky, so the gulls swoop in great waves, lifting like veils to glide back and forth in the air, their frames iridescent in the light, lifting then settling, then lifting again. They rarely move further away. In the deep night the sea is the loudest thing I can hear, the waves smashing down on the shore, as if it enjoys this timeout as well, when very few of us are mucking around near or inside of it.

A recent Griffith University research project, which applied a methodology of well-established studies in the economic contributions of outdoor sports to local economies, put the dollar value on a single surf break at South Stradbroke Island to the Gold Coast at over thirty million dollars a year. At one point, not accounting for economic downturns and fluctuations, surfing was recognised as contributing to nine percent of economic activity in the city and eleven percent of employment.[7] But such data and reach appears to not have registered in the frontal lobes of this city's elite policymakers even though the council published a report on the findings on their website. In 2019, Mayor Tom Tate turned up to a Surf World Gold Coast museum event in a Hawaiian shirt with no idea who he was co-presenting or conversing with. In among a bevy of homegrown world surfing champions, he was the distant uncle with no clue. To the despair of everyone present, he fumbled his way through.

A Smooth Sea Never Made for a Skilled Sailor—Surfing, Healing and Philosophy

It's far too early on a Saturday morning when I get a text from Tim Baker saying he can get me into writers festival session he's speaking at that's supposedly sold out. (I'd wondered if it was still on given we were in what would prove to be the baby stages of the coronavirus lockdown.) My eyes want to go back to being stuck together but I throw off the covers and go, driving gingerly down the GC Highway to the Burleigh Heads Surf Club, pulling into the Broadbeach Maccas for a frozen coke—a foolproof bender mender. It's eight am and Burleigh is resplendent in all its high-voltage glory. Athleisure junkies walking in their blow-dried hair and high-performance tights. Maori families nabbing the best picnic tables already. Surfers weaving between the packed parked cars, boards under their arms. Hipsters in their man buns and fluro short shorts patterned with ironic bananas or pineapples or images of Che Guevara. Clumps of Rasta-looking hippies under the Norfolk pines looking like they haven't slept—and me, shades firmly on, because the sea is doing its endless stretch of sparkling glitter thing and the golden sunshine rolling over us all is almost too much. Almost.

The beautiful irony of attending a writers festival event in a surf club on the Gold Coast is not lost on me. A city where the worlds of literature and surfing are more synonymous than they are anywhere else in the country, two worlds which had defined my life in the mid to late '90s, that I'd worked so hard to keep separate—now well and truly enmeshed. And so here we are, eating our breakfast while the sea sparkles beyond the windows over Burleigh Point and the speakers take the floor, to talk about the transformative power of surfing, and the life lessons they've drawn from it.

There's my mate Tim Baker, a guy that's made a long and distinguished career out of writing about surfing; Gold Coast surfing legend and owner of one of the city's most popular surf schools Cheyne Horan; and Zara Noruzi (formerly Zarah Ghahramani) author of *My Life as a Traitor*, a woman persecuted for her activism by the Iranian government who found solace and healing in surfing.

She tells us, 'After I arrived in Australia, for me, the first time I stopped thinking about what had happened to me it was when I surfed for the first time, I was in the water, got the first wave and for the duration of that wave however long it was, I realised I hadn't been thinking about what had happened to me—it was like finding chocolate for the first time, I loved that feeling and I couldn't stop … that force is greater than you and what can happen to you.'

Tim opens with a Timothy Leary quote, a guy who turned dropping acid into a legitimate research pursuit, waxing lyrical about surfing—even back in the '60s he saw surfers not as the dregs of humanity or the black sheep but as the 'futurists':

> They are leading the way to where man ultimately wants to be. The act of the ride is the epitome of 'be here now', and the tube ride is the most acute form of that. Which is: your future is right ahead of you, the past is exploding behind you, your wake is disappearing, your footprints are washed from the sand. It's a non-productive, non-depletive act that's done purely for the value of the dance itself. And that is the destiny of man.[8]

When Tim finishes, a collective silence descends on the room—we all recognise just how profound those words have proven to be. Acid-induced maybe but tuned in to a sense of existence humanity is *still* trying to get right over fifty years later. Sensing the moment, Tim says, 'Well that about sums it up, thanks for coming everyone,' and we all crack up.

The interplay between surfing, philosophy and art has never been that distant. Tim points out how much surfing culture has infused music, film, literature and visual art particularly since the 1960s when countercultural movements introduced notions of consciousness-raising to the mainstream. I think of my second year at university when artist Tracey Moffatt came to speak to us.

She was in town making video artwork, a spliced-up collection of street scenes shot in secret, male surfers dressing and undressing in beachside carparks, that would become her seminal work *Heaven* (1997). I remember the heady eroticism of the images, white towels tucked firm around washboard waists or slipping off, bronzed torsos cut and rippling, an inversion of the male gaze. As the film goes on, Tracey gets closer and closer to her subjects, a voyeuristic charge that becomes more of an interaction. I'm reminded too of the lurid cool of hometown boy Scott Redford's GC-inspired paintings: silhouettes of high-rises and palm trees against splashes of neon yellow, purple and hot pink skies, and his surf paintings which turn the literal materials of surfboards into abstract art. As I write this, I can see the nine-metre-high bright-red Stuart Green sculpture *All Eyes on Us* from my balcony, an arresting piece of public art rendered in plastic-coated glass that looks as if a giant had placed an origami flower made out of surfboards on the Esplanade.

Today, ideas linking surfing to consciousness-raising and so-called 'woke' culture are experiencing a resurgence as environmental concerns gain ascendency with attitudes towards self-care and healing emerging as directly linked. People are getting better at drawing the connection between their own mental and physical health and the sustainability of the planet. The very new-millennium surfing magazine *White Horses* was born on the Gold Coast and exemplifies this shift towards recognition of the implicit connection between artistic and philosophical ideas and surfing—not as a side salad but as the main meal. The recent edition, themed 'Take a Moment', is an easy sell—quotes from thinkers and musicians, writers and mystics, an eclectic pool from Annie Proulx to Archie Roach, to Homer and Spike Milligan, all in a high-gloss, high-design format where photography is still the hero but the language is sophisticated and big-picture, the images tagged with an accompanying Spotify playlist. A collectable item that reads like the future.

Cheyne Horan's connection to surfing is also linked to healing. When one of his best friends was killed, surfing was the only thing that made him feel better. It didn't make what had happened disappear, he says, he couldn't absolutely block it out in the purity of the moment as Zara was able to, but surfing helped him deal with it. When Cheyne tells us this story he's overcome with emotion—he is, in his words, still devastated, and even though the way his body is wracked with breath kind of undoes what he just said about surfing alleviating the pain, we believe him. Tim reaches out and rubs his back. A few of us in the audience make sympathetic noises. You can't help it. The vibe in the room has shifted. The fact that this world champion surfer is sitting at a table at nine in the morning and just letting those emotions loose is not what I expected. If there's a cardboard cut-out of a typical Aussie bloke or an old-school surfer, Cheyne would be it. With his open tanned face, big square head, nondescript T-shirt and boardies vibe he looks like *that* guy. But as his stories spool out, his unfiltered nature and eccentricities start to show. He tells us about the second time he experienced a healing in relation to surfing.

'I had an accident in Hawaii, I tore my shoulder almost like a chicken bone, pulled the bone off the muscle. I took off on a giant wave in Hawaii, I was the only guy in the water, I took off and the wave was throwing over the front, throwing over the back and I'm out there in the dark, I used to go out in the black just to try to get it alone, and there's no way out of this wave so I've jumped off and I've gone bang into the wave and its lifted my arm up here.' He gestures to the ceiling. 'Back then, now they wear life jackets and stuff, we had no way—how do you get out of a big-wave situation? I've just made it up on the spot, I'm gonna jump in, burrow a little hole and go into the face of the wave, this thing's just torn my arm, underneath the water I've torn my rotator cuff, come up, board's in two pieces, I come to the beach.

'Now, I'm in America. I can't go to the hospital or it's gonna cost me ten grand just to walk in the door, and I'm a surfer living off brown rice and beans. So I go to this Hawaiian kahuna, I go and see Maui and I tell him what's happened and he says, "Look Cheyne, Hawaiians in the old days would go and we'd put the broken part underneath the level of the earth and the earth would heal it." And

I said, "Oh okay that sounds alright."' The room erupts in laughter, it's as if all of these things are just normal or entirely possible to Cheyne, he's willing and open to anything.

'So I go onto the beach I dig this massive hole, I put my arm in, and it's just ruined, I put my arm underneath and I'm about that far underneath the earth and I'm lying there on Sunset Beach just watching the guys surf when all of a sudden the arm just started to throb, right? And I thought, Oh wow that must be it, that's the thing. So anyway, it healed my arm.'

In my head I'm like everyone else in the room right now, wanting to get up and go dig a hole in the beach and lay my body down in it. You heal your heart in the sea and you heal your broken bones in the ground.

Every single surfer I spoke to when researching this story spoke about similar effects. Without fail. It wasn't just that surfing was physically good for them, that they kept fit or that the focus required meant they were able to switch off—surfing was time out, from lives and responsibilities and a kind of active solitary meditation, sure, but the experience was also something else, something more ephemeral, something to do with force. Zita had talked to me about *sympatheia*, an idea she had read about in Ryan Holiday's book *Ego Is the Enemy*. In the text, he draws on French philosopher Pierre Hadot's descriptions of 'oceanic feeling'—a sense of belonging to something larger, of realising that:

> human things are an infinitesimal point in the immensity. It is in these moments that we're not only free but drawn toward important questions: Who am I? What am I doing? What is my role in this world? Nothing draws us away from those questions like material success— when we are always busy, stressed, put upon, distracted, reported to, relied on, apart from. When we're wealthy and told that we're important or powerful. Ego tells us that meaning comes from activity, that being the centre of attention is the only way to matter. When we lack a

connection to anything larger or bigger than us, it's like a piece of our soul is gone. Like we've detached ourselves from the traditions we hail from, whatever those happen to be (a craft, a sport, a brotherhood or sisterhood, a family). Ego blocks us from the beauty and history in the world. It stands in the way.[9]

When Cheyne starts launching into another story about the healing power of surfing, I can tell he's really building up to something, so I lean in. The story starts off fairly nondescript—one of his mates emerging out of the water at Burleigh with a look of pure joy on his face. That expression had gotten Cheyne thinking. He sat down on the beach and thought and thought and then, bam—he'd had an epiphany.

'What makes you feel so good when you go in the ocean?' he asks us like we're in some kind of evangelistic show on late-night TV and he's really getting into it. 'There's something more than just the positive ions. It's more. When you go in the ocean, right? And you are actually in the ocean, not a swimming pool—the ocean—when you go inside the ocean you are actually inside the planet.' When the room erupts into nervous giggles he says, 'It's pretty spacey isn't it?' But he keeps pushing the point, like he knows this for sure, like he's trying to convince us.

'It's real. That's it … and you guys have all experienced this, when you actually immerse yourself completely in the ocean, you can't breathe, you are not in oxygen, you are now inside the planet. And that's where the healing is. It's in there.'

When I get home from the event, I get changed and wrangle together the things I need for a typical session on the beach: books, pens, notepads, fruit, water, maybe a sneaky flask full of vodka and bitter orange, in case, as the afternoon stretches, the mood takes me. I'm looking forward to getting wet and getting healed. Despite COVID-19, the beaches aren't yet officially closed, and the sand is peopled as it usually is with faces from all over the world—the Brazilian, Indian, French, Cuban, Spanish and Middle Eastern backpackers who haven't yet scurried home or can't afford to, accents and beats from portable speakers pealing out around me. The perfect kind of swell for swimming just beyond the break, the waves all bulbous and rolling soft, the wind behaving, the water so clear and fresh my skin is a glass and I'm the Schweppervescence. Going under and opening my eyes to give them a good clean-out, blinking at the immensity of this thing I'm in, that I can't see much of beyond the bubbling wash and shadows. Catching wave after wave until I'm out of breath and floating on my back, toes pointing towards the shore, staring at this crazy beautiful beast of a city I call home, glossy towers piercing a sky so blue and cloudless it's almost criminal, a small bream brushing past me, the sun peaking.

The Gold Coast and its surfing culture have had their summits and troughs, waves of brilliance and triumph, countered by falls from grace when the players have crashed down on the jagged rock of parochialism—tired sloganeering, old ideologies, old ways. This period of ambassadorship we're in might feel a little over-designed sometimes, too white-linen and squeaky-clean to be believed, but surf culture is thriving and this blossoming is representative of the kinds of shifts I've witnessed in other subcultural facets of the Gold Coast, particularly the arts scene, a scene that once felt like a Petri dish, now burgeoning and spreading.

What has changed is an on-the-ground feeling that maybe we don't have to hide from what we've always known is so special about this place. The waves are cresting. A lot is going to depend on how well we protect the immensity and fragility of the oceanic environment we're so privileged to be paddling around the edges of, how much we push back against path dependence and save the city from itself.

I know the first thing I'm gonna do when all this isolation bullshit is over is book a lesson at surf school run by Cheyne Horan, a guy who knows in his bones that one of the best things we can all do for ourselves is to get inside the planet.

The Sea: Friend or Foe?

Emily Brugman

The water is blue and clear and serene. Here at Iluka, in the Northern Rivers region of New South Wales, the swell ricochets off the breakwall and bounces back towards the sandbank sidelong, allowing itself be reshaped, moulded into a perfect playful wedge. When it hits the sandbar fully, it pitches, and the belly of the ramp drops out from underneath. As I'm picked up and catapulted down the face of a mini Iluka bowl, I'm mystified by the whole scenario. That this moving ball of liquid energy converged with the earth here and now, tripping over the sudden rise in the seafloor, picking me up and taking me with it. It's a small day at Iluka, but the locals nevertheless hold their ground. This is a leisurely Saturday-morning surf, a routine head-wetting to get the weekend started. As I wait for another wave, I look back at the rip rushing out alongside the breakwall, a reliable lift from shoreline to line-up. The more time we spend in the ocean, the better we learn to work with the movement of water, rather than against it. But even the most experienced among us have found ourselves in trouble. The sea gurgles and surges at the base of the boulder-made wall, and I imagine surfer Mick Campbell's body floating there, in the boil and spume of white water. What would I have done, I wonder, had I been in his partner's position? The surf was much bigger that day. A junky north-east swell marching diagonally into the wall. I shudder knowing just how quickly a routine head-wetting can turn dreadfully wrong.

In his memoir *Land's Edge*, Tim Winton writes, 'I love the sea but it does not love me'.[1] For many of us, going to the sea is a daily ritual akin to prayer. An act both vital and necessary to the healthy function of body and mind. We think of the sea as a dear, dear friend, but the ocean has many faces. The sea is a place where the magnificence of life is brought to bear by the ever-present notion of death. Throughout the ages, seafaring tales have told of explorers going to the edges of the known world and returning somehow changed. I'm thinking of the characters of Homer's *Odyssey*, Melville's Captain Ahab and many of Winton's more modern protagonists. In all of these tales, the sea is a space of paradoxical forces, of both death and destruction, of freedom and renewal. The real sea, too, is a positive and negative space, an entity that gives and takes in equal measure. In my exploration of the sea as friend or foe, I came across real-life modern seafarers—swimmers and sailors and surfers—who have experienced the sea in all its extremes, and like the characters of those seafaring stories, they too have come back altered. These are the extraordinary stories of ordinary people who have answered the call of the wild.

The Swimmers

As a surfer, I like to consider myself a water-woman of sorts, someone who lives in close proximity to nature, who understands the ebb and flow of water. But as I sit, perched on my surfboard at Wategos, a small cove at the tip of Cape Byron, 120 kilometres north of Iluka, I know deep down that I am not the real deal. I am familiar with the view above the waterline, I can read the movement of water from above, but the liquid world below remains a mystery to me. Sometimes I think I'd rather not know exactly what goes on down there. In the case of the surfer, isn't ignorance a kind of bliss? Way out past the break, I can see four swimmers moving across the bay in unison. Ever since the spate of shark encounters that took place in and around Byron Bay between 2014 and 2016, grey suits have never been far from my mind. It's surprising to me that people have never stopped swimming this route. At the very least, on a surfboard you can swing around and catch the next wave in. Those swimmers out there, they are braver than I am.

Later, I learn that this tight-knit group of four women are between sixty-three and seventy-three years old, and have been swimming the bay at least twice a week for over two decades. Anne, Christine, Clare and Jill have a very special bond with the sea, and with one another, forged over almost seventy years of collective experience in these waters. I want to know why they do what they do, and how they manage their anxieties when swimming in the sea. Can the ocean ever really be a trusted friend? It's time for a deeper kind of immersion, I tell myself, and I swallow my fear when I ask these women if they will take me along on one of their ocean swims. They politely agree, and my stomach is shot with butterflies.

Anne, Christine, Clare and Jill came to swimming for different reasons.

'It's a healing process,' says seventy-three-year-old Christine, the oldest of the four women. She seems to be the glue of the group, the one that brought them together, and into the sea. 'Clare had a terrible breakup,' she says, eyeing her friend. Clare gives a small nod: go ahead. 'I said, "Come swimming." And that's how it started.'

'And Anne,' continues Christine, 'she had a horrific car accident. "Come swimming," I said. And she did. When she first came she couldn't dive down, because her hips were compromised. Now, we have to drag her off the bottom.'

Swimming for these women is more than exercise—it is a cathartic process, a ritual, a communal experience.

'It's exercise with awe,' Jill tells me.

'And you meet the most beautiful animals,' adds Christine. 'To be able to meet wildlife, to be eye to eye, on the same level ...'

This is the beauty of swimming in the sea, I think, as compared with riding waves on its surface, as I do. It is a deeper, steadier, more unhurried experience. The sea is a friend, these women assure me, even if they have encountered their fair share of fearful moments.

On the morning of my swim, the sky is filled with smoke haze. It's summer 2019, and half of New South Wales is ablaze. Everything is blanketed in a soft sepia hue, and I think it's strange how beautiful disaster can look. The sea is opaque, a silky grey. Perhaps it's not the best day for an ocean swim? This is one of the rare occasions that Anne is absent, and I have a feeling I will prove a bumbling replacement. We don our flippers and snorkels and wade into the water. A wave breaks on the shore and I find myself toppling over in the shallows, unbalanced and clumsy in my flippers. Christine asks if I'm okay, and I hide my embarrassment beneath a toothy grin. I'm less adept here, among swimmers, than I am in the line-up on my surfboard. I wonder if they are having second thoughts about bringing me along. There have been a few failed attempts over the years—people who have wanted to take part in this morning pilgrimage and haven't been able to go the distance. I plunge out through the shore break and into a blizzard of tiny brown particles. The *Colpomenia*—better known as cornflake seaweed—is common for springtime, but the scale of this year's bloom is unprecedented. In overarm, we begin sifting through the muck, heading south. As we go, I consider the fact that I can't see more than a foot in front of me. A small shiver runs through my body as I think of all the things that could be lurking around me. I swim on, and it's like feeling my way through a strange house in darkness. At around the five-hundred-metre mark we pause to take stock of our position. Each woman checks in on me.

'Are you comfy?' asks Jill, and I say yes, even though it's not completely true.

I orientate myself, taking in the sheer headland on one side, and the open sea on the other. Way out ahead, I see the rock formations of Nguthungulli. Most people know them these days as Julian Rocks, a popular destination for snorkelling and diving, some three kilometres out from Byron Bay's main beach. For the local Arakwal people, these rocks are the resting place of Nguthungulli, grandfather of the earth, who settled here and turned to stone after creating the land and the waters.[2] This band of coastline has been known for its beauty and fertility since time immemorial. Rich with both sea and bush tucker, there are Indigenous meeting places and camp sites dotted along the shorelines. Behind me, on the other side of the cape, there is a long, wild beach reaching south to Broken Head. A dreaming story tells of three sisters swimming off the headland there:

> The youngest sister swam out and became caught in a treacherous current flowing between the rocks. Her older sisters swam to save her but were also swept out. The three of them became exhausted fighting against the current and drowned, becoming the rocks that carry their name.[3]

The three magnificent rock formations, known to the Arakwal as one entity—the Three Sisters Rock—punctuate the headland at Broken Head, and no doubt contribute to the sandbanks that appear there every so often, creating a shapely right-hand point break. But a strong rip travels out along those rocks, and the water on the other side of the outcrop is deep and dangerous. The story of the three sisters was told as a warning to Arakwal children to discourage them from swimming there, lest they too drown and turn to stone. A swim in the sea can, after all, change from something lovely and pleasant to something nightmarish in a matter of moments, as it did for Clare.

We continue to tread water, and Clare points landwards, to the sheer rock face jutting out of the sea.

'That's where it happened,' she says.

A few years ago, the swimmers found themselves being pushed, suddenly and unexpectedly, towards the steep rocky headland that separates Wategos from The Pass. Strong northerly winds and persistent swells pressed the women into this worrying position, and while Christine and Jill managed to scramble up onto smaller rocks and clamber to higher ground, Clare was left struggling at the base of a high, vertical boulder.

Clare recounted this chilling scenario on the first day we met.

The group had just returned from their morning swim, and we settled down to talk and sip coffee on the grassy hillock overlooking Wategos.

'I couldn't get a foothold,' she told me. 'The sand was out, the water was very deep, and the waves were pushing in to sheer cliff face. It was really scary.'

'You were drowning,' stated Christine.

'It was a real life and death situation,' admitted Clare, 'because with each wave I would get picked up and then pulled underneath.'

'You thought you were going to die,' added Christine.

'I definitely thought I was going to die.'

'And I was watching my beautiful friend,' said Jill, 'and I couldn't do anything. So I was just going, "Don't you dare give up. Don't you dare give up!"'

Miraculously, a passerby had noticed the women being washed in against the rocks, and had picked his way down the headland from the top end.

'Somehow he got around the crevice,' said Jill incredulously. 'A strong, beautiful man. I called out to Clare, "Someone's coming!" and she didn't believe me.'

'I just couldn't believe there could be someone there.'

The man—Clare's saviour—somehow managed to pluck her out of the water and ferry her to safety. To scale the rock face as he did—he must have found superhuman strength in that moment.

'We were torn, Jill and I; we were shredded, legs bruised,' Clare told me.

'We shouldn't have gone that day,' conceded Jill, 'and now, we wouldn't go in those conditions.'

'We went back recently,' said Christine. 'Just to go back.' She didn't need to explain it further. I understand why they went back, although I don't know if I can articulate it. There is something to be said about returning to the scene of trauma.

'So friend or foe?' asked Jill, after a moment of introspection. 'I think that story encapsulates more than the fear of sharks. That was our most fearful moment.'

We continue on our way, hugging the coastline as it bends into The Pass. I see the heads of surfers—my people—bobbing up and down with the incoming swells. I pine for the yellow sandbank, shimmering gloriously beneath their feet. But we swim on, towards a reef in the middle of the bay. It is on this stretch that I feel the most exposed, the most vulnerable. It is deep, and we are a long way from the shore. Sharks circle at the edges of my imagination, but there is nothing to do but chase those thoughts away.

Christine has been surfing and swimming at Wategos for forty-five years. She arrived in the area when Byron Bay was still a blue-collar town, home to the Norco meatworks, the piggery and sand mining. Whaling off Belongil Beach was a recent memory.

'The place was full of sharks then,' Christine told me, 'because of the meatworks. The blood line came out into the sea. Every shop in town had sharks' teeth in the window. It was a very different town.' According to Christine, a period of tranquility followed the town's transformation, and for many years, she didn't give sharks a second thought, until 2015 came around, and the bubble burst.

'The bay is this magic place,' said Christine, 'and when that happened, it was like this magic circle got broken. I always sort of thought of the bay as this lovely balloon of safety, and it popped.'

For Homer and the ancient Greeks, the ocean served as an intermediary between the world of the living, the dead and the gods,[4] a concept that is shared among many cultures and mythologies. In Greek cosmology, the ocean is the locale of both paradise and hell, where one might come across the Islands of the Blessed or, for the less fortunate, the entrance to Hades. Those of us who frequent the sea today are aware of its paradoxes, and for many, sharks represent one of its darker, more unsettling sides.

In 2014, a fifty-year-old British man was swimming off Clarkes Beach, directly towards the shore from our current location, when he was attacked and killed by a great white shark. This was the attack that hit closest to home for Anne, Christine, Clare and Jill. Just five months later, in February 2015, Japanese man Tadashi Nakahara was fatally attacked at Ballina's Shelly Beach. In the months following, several other frightening but non-fatal encounters with sharks were reported on the North Coast. Anxieties ran high, and the surfing population was shaken. Raucous meetings were held in which communities and perspectives clashed. Some called for the installation of shark nets and drum lines, as well as culling, while others were strongly opposed to such measures. Many surfers stayed out of the water, while others took pleasure in unusually empty line-ups.

Anne, Christine, Clare and Jill continued swimming. They did not miss a single session, which I find unbelievable. But they have changed the way they do things, to some extent, mitigating the risks where they can.

'We've got these,' Jill said, showing me what looked to be a watch. It's a shark deterrent magnet, worn around the ankle. 'We're not sure if they work or not,' she continued. 'We've been told they probably don't.'

'We swim on Saturday and Sunday mornings, after eight when the helicopter has come by,' added Christine. 'And I check the app—the shark sightings app—every morning before we go. We're not completely stupid! We did some research. We've got the helicopter, the app, we've got our magnets, and if we get done, we get done.' She said it matter-of-factly. *If we get done, we get done.* This is a risk they are willing to take, for the reward that comes with it. I can understand this. At the height of the shark hysteria, I continued to surf, as most people did. I kept away from certain areas, like river mouths, and avoided going out in the early morning or the late evening, but the prospect of staying out of the water completely never really occurred to me. And I have to admit, these cautionary tactics have slowly fallen away.

'I'd rather live with fun in life than not do it,' said Christine, echoing my thoughts exactly. 'Besides, we love wild animals, they're phenomenal. I mean, what's wrong with a wild animal? They are things that we can't control, but it's good for us. That's life, that's nature. You can't control it, you have to be in it. It's better to be in it, isn't it?'

I'm learning that swimming in the sea is about letting go of control, about accepting your animal nature. I try to remember this as we cut across the trough between The Pass and the outer reef.

It goes on and on.

The nothingness finally turns to coral, and all of a sudden I am swimming above a shallow reef. It's not like the iridescent, vibrantly coloured reefs of the north, but it has its own secrets and hidden gems. I spot a loggerhead turtle paddling beneath me and my fear fades, overtaken by curiosity.

We come to a significant point in our journey: before heading off, Jill mentioned the bright yellow pad of coral, a marker of sorts. It helps the swimmers take stock of their whereabouts on the reef, but it is more than a signpost.

'We do this thing,' Jill said, 'where we always dive down and touch it.'

The women go, one by one, to give the yellow sponge its ritualistic tap. Should I too, I wonder? But it feels somehow wrong, like this ritual belongs to them, and I'm an imposter. To touch the yellow coral would be like standing to receive the bread of Christ without having completed communion.

As we hover patiently above the reef, their friends slowly come out of hiding. We see many gold-tinged wrasse and a tiny, three-spotted *Dascyllus* fish. I'm told that this area is unique because the tropical and temperate currents meet here, resulting in a huge variety of marine species coming through.

'Because we swim over the reef so often,' said Jill, 'I know that landscape better than I know any other bit of land anywhere really … And some things are in the same spot for years.' According to Jill, there is a group of basslets that hangs around in one particular location, year in, year out. There are the reliable crayfish, and the clown triggerfish, who shelters in a hole on the outer reef, with whom Jill has struck up a special visiting relationship.

Now, a plodding blue groper inspects us inquisitively. Its friendly, thick lips and blue colouring makes me think of playdough. A little way off, Clare points out an eagle ray fluttering freely above the reef bed. I am struck by its elegance. Earlier, Clare recalled a moment swimming amongst these beautiful creatures.

'We all came together and swam above four eagle rays,' she told me. 'We were there, they were there. We were four and they were four, and we just felt ...'

Her sentence petered out, perhaps because it was a difficult feeling to describe. But that's what it's all about, I think, imagining this mirror image of women and rays, flying through water. It is about friendships, not only with each other but with animals. It is about feeling yourself as part of the universe, and understanding that you are not so different to other species, be they water- or land-dwelling creatures. It is a recognition of the majesty of your fellow earthlings. In Winton's 1984 novel *Shallows*, young Queenie Cookson hears the songs of whales in her dreams, and they become the intimation of God: 'I was only a little girl. I heard the voice of God calling from down in the bay ...'[5]

In this story, says academic and essayist Bill Ashcroft, 'whales are the epitome of the oceanic ... with strong links to both *Moby Dick* and the biblical story of Jonah'.[6] For Queenie Cookson, and for the swimmers, the marine world provides a pathway to something bigger and beyond the self.

Free diver and essayist Michael Adams suggests that immersion through swimming and diving offers a deeper connection to the planet's basic processes. Adams describes being underwater, how the 'suck and swell of the tides feel like the planet breathing'.[7] Our bodies begin to align with those long-forgotten rhythms of water, he says, a state of being vaguely familiar to all humans, having spent the first nine months of our lives floating in amniotic fluid. According to Adams, diving is not about discovery, but about the recovery of our 'embodied knowledge'.[8]

On that first morning at Wategos Beach, as the sun made its arc across the eastern sky, my conversation with the swimmers began to draw closer to the essence of the act.

'It's about freedom too, isn't it?' said Christine. 'You haven't got that gravity pull on you.' This is the feeling that Winton's characters so often experience. It's in the pool or in the surf that Queenie Cookson feels 'strong and quick and graceful', but in class she feels heavy, thinks herself 'dull and plodding'.[9] As Ashcroft writes, water is the 'medium of freedom' in Winton's novels, allowing people to 'feel the lightness of their being'.[10] This is surely the element of the sea that keeps us returning, time and again, despite the threat of leviathans or even near-drowning experiences. Ashcroft goes on to say that Winton uses water 'to detect the holiness of the world, best encountered in the weightless brilliance of the sea',[11] and these swimmers, I think, ascribe to a similar notion.

'I think about how we repeat the same thing over again,' said Jill, 'and I'm an atheist, so I have no sense of what religion necessarily brings to people, but, for us, [swimming] is about ritual, it's about community, it's about immersion. Without trying to put a layer on it that we don't usually, there is something really deeply spiritual about it ... or something that I think other people are looking for in other things.'

Perhaps it is this feeling of being a part of something eternal, I think now. What Sigmund Freud called 'something limitless, unbounded—as it were, something "oceanic"'.[12] For those of us who do not call ourselves religious, water certainly offers a passage into something bigger, something timeless, and perhaps even sacred. It may speak to what Luce Irigaray calls the 'sensible transcendental'. 'Why do we assume that God must always remain an inaccessible transcendence rather than a realisation—here and now—through the body?' she asks.[13] We've all had quasi-spiritual moments in the surf, when we feel ourselves, for one wild moment, in the throes of nature, and everything else falls away. And more often than not, we emerge somehow renewed. For those who spend their lives in and on the water, Ashcroft suggests, the experience is one of constant renewal: 'the renewal of beauty and grace, the renewal of the miracle of life. It is the continual revelation that the world is holy'.[14]

We turn to go, my baptism complete, and begin making our

way back across the deep trough to the safety of The Pass. Despite the beauty and the freedom and the exquisite creatures we have met, there is a part of me that is grateful that this is coming to an end. I can't wait to get there—to my comfort zone, to dig my toes into the sweet, sweet grainy sand. I swim and swim and do not look back.

The Sailor

If there's mysticism in immersion, I wonder what possibilities lie beyond the shoreline. Boats were in my family, but I don't know the open sea. My migrant grandfather was a cray fisherman on the Abrolhos Islands. He used a compass to navigate and looked to the sky for his weather forecasts. Me, on the other hand—I stick to the coastal fringes, chasing waves rather than fish, and look to my smart phone for the forecast. Despite his legacy, the open ocean remains unfamiliar to me, and when I imagine being out there in the wide expanse, with no suggestion of land in sight, I prickle with unease. I want to know what motivates people to go to sea, and what it is they find out there.

Tony Mowbray is sixty-four, and has been on the water all his life. He began sailing on Lake Macquarie, his home turf, at age eleven, and had his first foray into the open ocean at age fourteen. He's agreed to talk me through his experience of the sea, which is no ordinary tale. At Nords Wharf, on the New South Wales Central Coast, we walk barefoot to the shoreline, where Tony rolls a dinghy over onto its right side, and pushes it easily into the clear blue lake water. In the still morning, we row out towards his prize possession—*Solo Globe Challenger*—the forty-three-foot yacht in which he has spent some of the best, and worst, times of his life.

We climb over the side of the boat and settle into bench seats on the deck. As the boat rocks gently to and fro, there's a stillness that settles around us. People go to sea for many reasons. For some it's the challenge posed by the elements, for others it's the restorative quality of water.

Earlier, as we drank coffee together at Tony's place, his daughter Holly told me that Tony has a lot of fire in him, and water soothes him. Perhaps for Tony the reasons for going to sea are more instinctual. It's a necessity, even.

From the moment Tony ventured onto open ocean, he was hooked. 'There's this magical feeling which is difficult to put into words,' he tells me, describing the calming, fluid quality of sailing. 'The sensory thing of water. That allure, it's like an addiction, once you're bitten, once you discover it, you can't go back.'

By the time Tony was eighteen, he had undergone the obligatory initiation of any serious Aussie sailor, participating in his first Sydney to Hobart Yacht Race. But it would be another one, many years later, that would prove his most memorable.

Anyone who is old enough will likely remember that the 1998 Sydney to Hobart went terribly and irrevocably wrong. Skipper Tony Mowbray, along with seven mates—Dave Cook (Cookie), Keir Enderby, Dave Marshall, Keith Molloy, Glen Picasso (Cyril), Tony Purkiss (Biggles) and Bob Snape—set off from Sydney Harbour that year bracing for strong winds and stormy conditions, but what they encountered was far more extreme than anyone anticipated.

The area of the boat is smaller than I imagined, and I struggle to see how eight men could inhabit it with any degree of comfort. But more than that, I can't quite imagine being stuck on the high seas atop this relatively small piece of fibreglass.

A number of elements came together that year to create the perfect storm. The East Australian Current (EAC), Tony tells me, runs from the equator down the east coast of Australia at varying speeds throughout the year, and its pace is directly related to the temperature of the ocean. In 1998, the water temperature in December was like bathwater—a blissful twenty-seven degrees Celsius—and as a result, the EAC was hurtling south at an almost unprecedented speed of four knots. The entire fleet was being catapulted south along with this current, and fourteen hours after the start time, all yachts were tracking ahead of the race record.

Meanwhile, to the south, a storm was brewing. When the EAC hit the relatively shallow Bass Strait, Tony says, it had to heave itself up and over the shelf, where it came head to head with a powerful low pressure system.

'When the waves generated by sixty knots of wind clashed headlong with four knots of East Australian Current moving in exactly the opposite direction that, additionally, was very busy trying to heave itself up over the shallower water of the Strait, then a massive collision of nature took place.'

What ensued was the most disastrous forty-eight hours in the history of the Sydney to Hobart, during which six men died and five yachts were lost to the sea. As the *Solo Globe Challenger* hit the Bass Strait, Tony and his crew met the first monumental wave that would ultimately bring them unstuck:

'The waves were coming through in sets, just like they do at the beach,' Tony tells me. 'In this instance it was the third wave in the set that was the biggest. We saw a set coming towards us, and the second wave in the set did two things: we reared up it, and as we came down, it set us back on our haunches, which meant we lost all our speed. Without speed, you lose all your manoeuvrability because you can't steer the boat. And then it slewed us around so that we were side-on. And anyone will tell you that when you're side-on to a wave, particularly of that magnitude, it can only mean one thing.'

It's an early lesson you learn in surfing: if you find yourself sidelong to a breaking wave you're going to get rolled. Tony describes the moment, at around four pm, with four men on deck and four men below, when the wave hit like a missile.

'Unless you've been hit broadside by a wave at sea you wouldn't know the feeling … It's like *ka-fucking-boom*, and over you go.'

The wave flipped the boat, and sent it tumbling down the other side of the crest. By the time it righted itself, around twenty long seconds later, all sorts of things had come to pass.

'The rope cavities have imploded and water has rushed into the cabin, the boat is in about three foot of water, the mast has broken off about six foot above the deck, it's laying out the side. Keir's legs are pinned by the rails and he's yelling out like a banshee. Cyril, who was steering the boat and was attached by his safety harness, has been thrown out the back and is being dragged along like a fishing lure, and now has a crushed rib cage. Keith has smashed his lower back, Biggles has snapped his leg just above the knee and has a head wound with massive amounts of blood coming down.'

Tony, who was in the cabin at the point of collision, climbed back up onto the deck, where he locked eyes with Cyril, who was still, remarkably, tethered to his harness off the back of the boat. 'He's looking straight at me, his eyes like dinner plates, and I'm like, "For fuck's sake Cyril, stop fucking around and get back on board will ya?"'

In the moments that followed, despite their injuries and the enormity of what had just transpired, Tony and his crew sprang into action. Most urgently, they needed to ditch the broken mast, which threatened to punch a hole in the boat.

'Second priority, get the water out.' Tony laughs when he tells me that the best bilge pump is a scared man with a big bucket.

Assessing their options, the group made a call to change course, thereby running with the wind and the waves, rather than against them. Now they headed east-north-east, tracking towards New Zealand.

'So we tried to pick our way through what you might call the minefield,' says Tony, 'very unsuccessfully at times.'

Biggles, with his broken leg, took up post as watchman. He was sitting beside Tony in the cockpit, looking back over the skipper's shoulder at the oncoming waves, which, due to their change in course, were now approaching from behind.

'You've got seventy- to eighty- foot waves and the top twenty-five foot of them is breaking white water. The waves were breaking irregularly and in sections. Biggles is going "Right, right, right. No, left, left, left!" I'm going, "For fuck's sake, Biggles, make up your mind!" Throughout that fifteen-hour ordeal there were so many waves that engulfed us, swamped us, rolled us, it just went on and on.'

I take a moment to consider seventy to eighty feet of dark water rising up behind you, but it's so far from my reality that it's difficult to conjure. I think of the butterflies welling in my belly when I see a humble four-footer rearing up to engulf me when I'm in the surf.

While Tony and his crew were trying their best to dodge these towering walls of water, several deep-sea waves still caught them unawares. With the swell approaching from the rear, *Solo Globe Challenger* found itself in the most unlikely position.

'I rarely talk about this wave because most people would say it's bullshit,' says Tony. 'The trouble is there were seven other blokes with me and they all know it's not bullshit. We got hit by this wave. It picked us up and slewed us onto our port side, and we started smashing across the face of the wave like a high-performance sailing dinghy, or like a surfboard. I crouched down on the starboard side of the cockpit and covered my eyes and mouth, thinking I'm going to get engulfed by water. After a while I'm thinking, What's going on? I'm not getting wet. I open my eyes up and we're in the tube of this wave.'

I look at Tony searchingly, but he is deadset serious.

'And the other guys will back you up on this?' I ask teasingly, 'because if no-one else saw it then it doesn't count ...'

'I know,' he says, 'it sounds unbelievable. Getting tubed in a forty-three footer. It is a pintail though.'

I wonder if *Solo Globe Challenger* is the only yacht to have found itself in that magical position? Then again, who knows what mysterious and outlandish things come to pass at sea? They didn't make it, though. A barrage of white water soon caught the boat sidelong and sent it tumbling, once more, down the face of the wave.

Amongst all the chaos, Tony was, somewhat surprisingly I think, able to feel awed by his surroundings. He recalls a moment looking back at the sea state behind him and thinking, Holy hell, have a look at this, just take this in, because you will probably never see anything like this ever again in your life. 'It was that off the dial,' he adds.

'What did you see?' I ask.

'Tumultuous walls of water, the top sections breaking all over the place, like vertical cliffs moving through the ocean hunting and seeking their prey. I couldn't possibly see how any form of rescue vehicle, whatever it was, by air or sea, could help you.'

This response is surely the upshot of a life spent on the sea, and the deep respect for nature that comes with it. I'm thinking of Melville's Captain Ahab, on day three of the chase, as he closes in on Moby Dick for the last time. In that moment, Ahab too, takes a moment to appreciate his backdrop:

> But let me have one more good round look aloft here at the sea; there's time for that. An old, old sight, and yet somehow so young; aye, and not changed a wink since I first saw it, a boy, from the sand-hills of Nantucket! The same!—the same!—the same to Noah as to me.[15]

Throughout the painstaking hours, Tony and his crew were made to confront the idea of death many times. In some moments, Tony was able to think about it from a relatively calm and contemplative standpoint: So, drowning, hey? Tony thought. I wonder what that will be like.

At other moments, they armed themselves with humour:

'Keith managed to roll a smoke. He rolls this big fat cigarette, because he reckons, "This might be my last one. I'm probably giving up after this, I'm not wasting any tobacco." So there were moments of humour,' Tony insists. 'There's gotta be.'

I ask Tony how the ordeal changed his relationships with the other blokes.

'The welding of those eight souls into one happened during that ordeal. It's cast into stone. The eight of us are as tight as tight. We don't necessarily speak to each other on a weekly basis but it's that thing of being able to pick up where you left off and heap shit on each other.' He grins, but then his expression changes, and he talks of a depth of camaraderie that many of us may never experience. 'It's actually a wonderful thing to be a part of. I feel very honoured.'

Again, I think of Ahab and his whalers:

> They were one man, not thirty. For as the one ship that held them all; though it was put together of all contrasting things—oak, and maple, and pine wood; iron, and pitch, and hemp—yet all these ran into each other in the one concrete hull, which shot on its way, both balanced and directed by the long central keel; even so, all the individualities of the crew, this man's valor, that man's fear; guilt and guiltiness, all varieties were welded into oneness, and were all directed to that fatal goal ...[16]

After fifteen long hours, Tony and his crew heard the *whomp whomp whomp* of a chopper, but by that time, the storm had spent its penny, as Tony put it.

'Did it feel good to hear the chopper?' I ask.

Tony hesitates, and I realise what a determined bastard he really is.

'Look, I got myself out there, I wanted to get myself home,' he tells me. 'It wasn't like the moment of salvation, but it was a pretty comforting noise to hear I gotta say.'

At this point, despite the arduous ordeal, Tony made a decision: he would not be abandoning ship. I'm incredulous. Seriously?

'We still had fifty-foot waves and fifty-knot winds but when you've had one-hundred foot and eighty knots, it's like, "How good is this?" It's all relative isn't it? You can get used to living in a forty-four-gallon drum with someone smashing it with a sledgehammer if you stay there long enough. You get a different perspective I guess, when you've been on the edge a bit.'

Three of the most seriously injured crew members jumped into the still-raging sea, which seems a terrifying act in itself, notwithstanding everything that had come before, and were airlifted to safety.

'There was a very quiet, sober moment after the chopper left,' says Tony. 'A period of contemplation. We were eight and now we were only five. But the conditions really started to calm down after that.'

A naval ship was sent out the following day, and Tony politely disobeyed orders to leave his boat.

'I wanted to get the yacht back through Swansea Inlet, tie it up at the Belmont Yacht Club and have a beer,' says Tony.

But this time around, Tony's picture-book homecoming wasn't to be. A trawler was sent out by his insurer. A deal was struck to get Tony and the remaining crew on board, and with the *Solo Globe Challenger* in tow, the trawler motored directly west, docking, at long last, at the far south coast town of Eden.

After stepping back onto solid land, Tony went on national television and said he was going to go home and mow the lawn and do a load of washing. He was going to abandon his plans to sail solo around the world. This seems like a logical reaction after an experience of this enormity. Except that he still had unfinished business with the sea. And that little niggling thought would only grow more prominent as the years wore on.

Less than a year later Tony had his boat fixed up, the mast remade, and was reconsidering the round-the-world trip.

'What changed?' I ask.

'When you're lying in bed at three in the morning and there's a black void going around and around and you just keep coming back to the same answer ... Well, that must be the answer, whether you like it or not.'

Not only did he complete that voyage, which involved spending one hundred days alone at sea, but by the time 2003 rolled around, the entire crew of the *Solo Globe Challenger* had agreed to have one more crack at the 'Hobart', 'to get the monkey off the back,' as Tony put it. In some cases, it seems that the call of the sea is just too loud to ignore.

Tony's is a tale of obsession not unlike that of Captain Ahab's, with both pitted against the elements. Ahab's epic quest for the white whale ultimately takes him to the murky depths of the Pacific: 'Towards thee I roll,' writes Melville, 'thou all-destroying but unconquering whale; to the last I grapple with thee; from hell's heart I stab at thee; for hate's sake I spit my last breath at thee'.[17] Throughout his years on the sea, Tony too seems to have rolled towards his own Moby Dick with some of the same vehemence and slightly obsessive enthusiasm. He tells me that one of the reasons he goes to sea is that he loves a challenge.

'When something goes wrong, I relish it. I love the challenge of, can I fix this problem? Those conditions [during the 1998 Hobart], in some perverted, twisted kind of a way, were a challenge to me.'

By the time we come to the end of *Moby Dick*, despite Ahab's dogged pursuit of the white whale, there is a sense that man, when set against nature, wages an impossible battle. Tony, too, concedes to the supreme power of the sea.

'Sometimes you'll hear people say "I tamed the sea", or "I beat it". You're never going to tame the sea. It's an entity all of its own, and it'll do with you what it wants to do. It'll swallow you up and spit you out in the blink of an eye if it wants to. It's your foe at times and it's your friend at times. It can be your worst enemy or your greatest asset. You gotta have respect for it.'

Indeed, as Melville suggests, the ocean is the only constant and enduring character in this story, and even after humanity's rise and collapse, 'the great shroud of the sea [will roll] on as it rolled five thousand years ago'.[18]

When Tony speaks about his solo voyage around the world, or the trips he's taken since, chartering boats from Patagonia to Antarctica, there's a lot more whimsy in his voice. These have been different kinds of experiences, where the magnificence has far outweighed the terror.

'What's the most beautiful thing you've seen on the sea?' I ask.

'Ah geez. Icebergs, whales, albatross that will just go with you for hours and hours and days and days ... Sunsets, stars. I used to go up on deck and look up from the cockpit at this jet-black velvet sky, at stars that look like diamonds that are gonna drip right out of the sky all over you. Then a plane would go over and you'd think, Ah those bastards up there eating their packets of peanuts!'

Just like the ocean swimmers, Tony is awed by his meetings with other creatures.

'To be eye to eye with a whale. It's spiritual. Down there they feed on krill. They'll come up with their mouths open and take in millions of krill at once. When they're in a feeding frenzy they're completely oblivious.' He grins. 'A bit like me when I'm chowing down, I don't want to know about anything else. You can get right here, this close.'

Tony gestures to the side of the boat and I imagine what that must feel like, to find yourself at arm's length from a creature of that ilk.

Captain Ahab's quest for Moby Dick has been seen by some as a metaphor for the spiritual search. So too Tony contemplates the possibility of a deeper meaning in the seafarer's journey, and like the ocean swimmers, the message he pulls from it is one of unity.

'People sometimes ask me, did I find God when I was out there? It's usually a believer and they'll yell out, "Did you find God?" Quite often I'll give them a smart answer like, "Oh, I didn't know I was supposed to be looking for him" or, "No, he's in a smaller boat, he's still coming" or, "Nah, he came second". The believers are deflated, but the non-believers love it, and hey, you can't please all the people all the time. But the true essence is that before I left to go around the world, my view was that it was us and them. Us being the intelligent ones, the human beings, and them being the animals, or everything else. And spending so much time out there in nature, I came home knowing it was just *us*.'

The search for meaning on the high seas is by no means a modern one. In her exploration of the sea in the Homeric verses, Marie-Claire Beaulieu notes that the sea is a space of divine epiphany and revelation.[19] The early prophetic god Proteus, god of rivers and oceans, is one of several deities that Homer calls the Old Men of the Sea, and embodies the elusive wisdom of nature.

Like water, Proteus has shape-shifting abilities. From this characteristic comes the adjective 'protean', meaning versatile, adaptable, or able to take on different forms. 'Lost sailors who cannot find their way in the moving, indeterminate space of the sea,' says Beaulieu, 'must hang on through the gods' metamorphoses in order to obtain a revelation concerning their way home'.[20] In the *Odyssey*, Menelaus is successful in holding onto Proteus through his violent transformations from lion to serpent, leopard to boar, water to tree, and thereby learns the truth about the fates of Agamemnon, Ajax the Lesser and Odysseus.[21] In this way, the Old Men of the Sea indicate more than a route to safety, but the greater knowledge gained through a journey into the unknown. Tony Mowbray and his crew certainly wrestled with Homer's shape-shifting divinities at various times during their horrific voyage, both physically and metaphorically, as they confronted their own mortality.

So how did round two of the Sydney to Hobart pan out?

'It was a very enjoyable race,' says Tony. 'It was a very different race from nineteen ninety-eight. We weren't there to win sheep stations, we were just there to complete the task. As you have probably ascertained by now, I'm big on finishing off what I started. I still remember that mental baggage, you know, that weight off my shoulders as we closed in on the finish line and that was very cathartic. Then that chapter of our life was closed and we could walk away.'

Unlike Ahab, Tony did not go down with Moby Dick, but he has had to grapple with the idea of his own mortality perhaps more than most.

'What's your attitude towards death now?' I ask.

'I still don't want to go,' he admits. 'I'm getting the shits because I'm sixty-four and I'm seeing all these things going on in the world and it's all just getting started. It's like fax machines came and went and now I gotta come and go. I'm resigned to the fact that I'll die, but for me it's a race to do all the things that I want to do before someone (my bank manager) or something (my health) stops me. You'll hear me saying things like: "You're here for a good time not a long time"; "This isn't a dress rehearsal". It's intensified my want to live and enjoy life, to get on with it and do stuff. You know, don't wait for tomorrow. Now's the time. And that was the ninety-eight Hobart.'

The yacht we're seated in now, the one in which those eight men rode to the edge of death and back again, has only recently come back into Tony's possession. He sold it several years ago, but like the loyal friend that it is, *Solo Globe Challenger* found its way home in due course. 'It was like my left arm,' Tony is quoted saying in the *Newcastle Herald*, of the connection to his sailboat.

Tony sailed the yacht from Italy, where it had ended up via a different owner, back to Belmont in 2019, and now that I know Tony better, I can see why this would have been a satisfying turn of events. Tony likes a story to come full circle, and bringing the boat home somehow feels like the right conclusion, considering everything they'd been through together. But it's not all smooth sailing from here on out. When you're a person of extremes, like Tony is, what makes you happiest in the world can also be your undoing.

'The answer to my question is always a boat,' he tells me. 'Why am I broke? It's a boat. Why am I downtrodden? It's a boat.'

I see that Tony's relationship with his boat, like his relationship with the sea, is a complicated one. He's on hiatus from sailing for the time being, and is renovating his home with the same gusto he usually reserves for the high seas. When I first called Tony to ask if he'd be part of this small interview series, I had mentioned that I was keen to talk about his relationship with the sea now, after all those years spent sailing and all the ups and downs. I'd laughed when he'd replied, 'It's a bit like Bunnings. I hate going there, but I go there three times a day.'

But there's more to it than that. He explains how the voice of caution has been growing louder in recent years:

'I'm getting older, and I'm starting to get more cognisant of how much it hurts when you fall over. I'm starting to get more wary of the sea.'

I think it's only natural to grow more careful with age. At some point in our lives, we come to realise our own vulnerability.

So what's next for Tony Mowbray?

'Ha! I might buy a pop-top caravan and go to the desert.'

On this I sense a shift in Tony. He is done with the interview and itching not to waste the remainder of the day. He has a reno to do. The oars lap softly as he guides them through the clear water on our way back to shore, where he turns the dinghy over on the bank. His movements are fluid and easy, long practised and, watching him, I am not so sure this sailor will be able to leave the water behind. I have been given glimpses of the fire in Tony that his daughter alluded to earlier, and if the elemental principles are anything to go by, he may crave that expanse of water as much as some of us need the comforting view of the shoreline.

The Surfers

Over the past months I've ventured deeper with the ocean swimmers, further with the sailor, and now it's time to get back to what I know. Mick Campbell and Tahlija Redgard are two people whose lives absolutely revolve around the ocean and surfing. I meet them at the lighthouse on the southernmost headland of Port Macquarie, and slip easily back into my old tongue—the language of surfing. They have pulled up to the carpark in their troopie, which doubles as their home. It's stacked to the brim with camping gear, fishing rods and surfboards. Tahlija's eyes are the crystalline blue of rockpools, and the smattering of freckles across her nose gives her a sandy, wistful look. She has her togs on, and her late grandfather's tattered flannelette shirt around her shoulders. Mick jumps out of the car and offers me a warm handshake. His face is slick with zinc from the morning's fishing, the lower half of it obscured by a dusty red beard. The few lines around his eyes suggest he smiles frequently. Mick and Tahlija's kelpie cross blue heeler, Tackle, will remain with the vehicle today.

Tackle doesn't have much contact with other people, they tell me. It keeps her focussed on the task at hand. She's a working dog with a different kind of job. Whenever her owners are absent—usually fishing or surfing—she stands watch over the troopie, which carries all of Mick and Tahlija's worldly possessions, most of which are of a practical nature. We leave her to it, and head down the northern face of the headland to find a patch of shade and a view of the ocean, which has a wild edge to it today.

Port Macquarie's own Mick Campbell rose to notoriety in the late '90s when he finished second to Kelly Slater in the world title race. Noted for his fiery determination and athleticism, Mick became known throughout the surfing world as the 'Ginja Ninja'. His partner, Tahlija Redgard, grew up further north, in the coastal town of Bundaberg. Her father was a keen surfer and small-scale fisherman, who sold the coral trout, mackerel and crayfish he caught to put the kids through school. Tahlija used to help the old man deliver his catch via pushbike after school. 'My mum is a Gunggari woman,' she tells me. Gunggari refers to the Indigenous people of southern Queensland, whose tribal lands centre around the Maranoa River, west of Brisbane. Mick and Tahlija met in Port Macquarie in 2012 and bonded over their shared passion for a life lived in and on the water. 'We've spent countless sleepless nights fishing off the rocks together,' Tahlija says. A classic surfing couple, they've been inseparable ever since.

In recent times they've garnered a small following through a handful of online clips, tracking their surfing adventures through Indonesia and the more remote coastal regions of Australia. But they are far from internet personalities. When I searched for Tahlija online, her social media profile announced: 'I don't use this. Email me.' It was some weeks before I received a reply because, as I came to understand, she's not someone who checks her phone too often. But Mick and Tahlija's freewheeling and adventurous life together took on a whole new dimension after a near-drowning incident at Iluka breakwall left Mick fighting for his life.

In 2017, Mick and Tahlija had just returned from a surf trip to the Mentawai Islands, where they had scored perfect double-overhead Kanduis—a fast, funnelling left that grows shallower and heavier as it moves down the line. They landed back on home soil with a renewed taste for challenging waves, and when they saw a swell building off the east coast they beelined it directly to Iluka breakwall. It had been raining for weeks and the Clarence River had swelled with the rising water. During floods, the briny river water runs through the breakwall and joins forces with the torrent of rip running out alongside it.

When Mick reflects on the conditions in the ocean that day, he acknowledges there were several elements that came together to create the chaos that followed.

'There were all these dynamics,' says Mick, 'looking back on it—kind of eerie dynamics. The water was dirty, so the waves looked quite angry. The swell was raw, six feet, maybe some eight-footers, and the direction was a little bit wrong. Ideally, it's best on a south-east swell. But on this day, it was east, coming straight at the wall and unloading on the sandbank, which was ruler-edged and beautiful. The sand was compact, like concrete, rock-solid and so shallow.'

Fatefully, the pull of that revelling swell prevailed, and Mick and Tahlija were out there.

But moments before they paddled out, Mick had an inexplicable urge to swap his leg-rope for a big-wave leash.

'The one I had on was fine,' he says. 'I'd worn it in Indo in ten- to twelve-foot waves, but I just had this feeling in my stomach that I needed to swap it over.' This off-the-cuff act may have helped to save his life, along with Tahlija's indomitable character.

Mick and Tahlija surfed the unusually empty beachie for almost three hours before it happened.

'We got a couple of good ones each, a couple of barrels,' says Tahlija. 'Like you could have parked a car in them hey, they were that wide and thick and heavy.'

'I had got a few crazy ones,' says Mick, 'and I think maybe I was in overdrive. But when you're a surfer, that's what you look for, you know, that feeling.'

I've got an inkling that the feeling Mick's describing is a different thing altogether to the pleasant, joyful sensation I'm looking for. 'Can you describe it?' I ask. 'That feeling you're chasing?'

'Maybe it's the feeling of making the unmakeable,' says Mick. 'Like, I shouldn't have made that but I did. It's so empowering for yourself.'

I think about this for a moment. About the possibility of defying reason, of defying the natural order of things.

'The rush,' he continues. 'It's kind of indescribable. At the time, it's like you're about to explode from the inside out. It feels like you are about to go *bang* with pure excitement and joy.'

'And all that's in your head is what's just happened,' adds Tahlija. They're really on a roll now.

'I've got goosebumps just thinking about it,' says Mick, 'because that's what we have as humans, that's our spirit. Your spirit is just so alive in that moment. It's hard to explain.'

Tahlija gives it a go.

'You paddle into a wave, and you're looking at it as you paddle into it, and you're thinking to yourself, there's no way I'm going to make this thing. Then you pull into it and you're not making it in your head the whole time, you're just driving through this thing, and you're behind the foam ball and then you feel this weightlessness as it spits you out. That weightlessness, it's almost like an infinity feeling.'

I'm reminded of Winton's character Sando, the troubled has-been surf legend from his novel *Breath*, who articulates it like this: '"When you make it, when you're alive and standin' at the end, you get this tingly-electric rush. You feel *alive*, completely awake and in your body. Man, it's like you've felt the hand of God".[22] Bill Ashcroft suggests that *Breath* is a story about 'asserting ... power [over your body] in various ways, of confirming existence itself by going to the edge of one's ability in what feels like a religious experience'.[23] Just like Sando and other characters in Winton's novels, Mick and Tahlija willingly take themselves to that precipice in order to feel alive.

As a fellow surfer, I could say I understand that feeling that both Mick and Tahlija so eloquently describe, but to be honest I'm not so sure that I do. I don't think I've been there, to the edge of things, like these two have, and I'm not certain I ever will.

'How do you manage the fear?' I ask. 'Are you afraid of the prospect of a long hold-down?'

'Mick told me this a long time ago: just open your eyes,' says Tahlija. 'When you're under the water, when you're vulnerable, open your eyes to the darkness and you'll be able to find your way up.'

Like her father, Tahlija is a proficient spearfisher, and I have no doubt that the hours she's spent underwater trailing fish have contributed to her comfort in big waves.

'Diving gives you a sense of peace and relaxation,' she tells me, 'and you feel that after a long hold-down too, I think. When you come up, you come up feeling relaxed. You feel that you've just been to the depths and you come back up and you almost feel euphoric.'

Tahlija is speaking to that same notion of embodied knowledge experienced by the ocean swimmers. As Michael Adams suggests, swimming and diving are 'simultaneously planetary and intensely intimate—the ocean is both all around us and within us', and the water, if we let it, will '[rock] the body into peace'.[24]

I return to Tahlija's description of a long hold-down, how it takes you to the depths (of what, I wonder?), and that euphoric feeling afterwards. I can't help but think she's reaching for that same idea the ocean swimmers had attempted to describe—that oceanic feeling.

In contrast to Tahlija's peaceful re-emergence, I think about the way I panic-scramble to the surface after a hold-down, heart racing, throat contracting, chest on the verge of bursting open. We are two very different beings. Even so, all of us as surfers spend much of our time in a liminal space: at the coastal fringes, somewhere between land and water. When we are underwater, swimming or diving or waiting out a hold-down, we also take our bodies to a threshold state, a border between one condition and another. When immersed in water, says Michael Adams, we find the space between breaths, between breathing and not breathing, between life and death. It is the metaphorical and physiological intersection between these two states of being, and I reckon Mick and Tahlija have spent more time in that space than most. Adams suggests that this state of liminality 'connects us to ancient stories in many cultures of mermen and mermaids: beings between human and water creature'.[25]

Back at Iluka breakwall that day, Mick and Tahlija continued to flirt with the unruly swells that marched towards them from the horizon. Then Mick took off on a wave and didn't paddle back out. A relentless set followed, and it wasn't until a few minutes had passed that Tahlija realised something was very wrong.

'There's always a rip on a breakwall and it takes a split second to get back out, no matter the size of the swell. I had this feeling in my stomach. Something bad has happened.'

Tahlija glimpsed Mick's board floating in the rip, and as she drew closer, the curved form of his back, clad in the familiar material of his wetsuit, poking out of the water.

'I grabbed him up and he was the bluest blue I'd ever seen. Purple-blue, almost black. Foaming from the mouth, blue lips, eyes wide open, but no-one there. Foam coming out of his nose. Just full to the brim with water.'

'What did you think in that moment?' I ask Tahlija.

'I was just like, fucken hell, this is my best friend. He's dying in my arms, he's dying right here. I was freaking out but I was also really focussed, you know. All I could think about was how I was going to save him.'

'What was your immediate reaction?'

'I was holding him up in the water, and I was screaming at him, "Come back, come back, there's nothing wrong with you! Come back." To me, and to the average eye, you would have thought he was dead for sure. He was completely lifeless.'

Tahlija held Mick's ragdoll body above water as best she could, while waves washed them up against the wall and the rip ran ceaselessly outwards. In an effort to revive Mick, Tahlija began banging him in the chest. 'I was punching him as hard as I could.'

At this point Tahlija noticed another person surfing on the next bank over. She called frantically for help, until the surfer, a young man of nineteen named Scott, paddled across to where she struggled, his eyes wide with fear. He held onto Mick while Tahlija continued the chest compressions which, when performed in the water, resembled something more like assault.

'I was telling him in his ear, "Wake up, there's nothing wrong with you, you're fine, there's actually nothing wrong here. Just wake up. We're here with you."'

'Were you lying?' I ask.

'Yeah,' she says, 'I guess I was. I wanted him not to be scared in his head, and not think he was going.'

A bubble escaped Mick's mouth, and sea water started pouring out. They decided now was the time to try and heave Mick onto a surfboard.

'The current is just like a river,' Tahlija tells me, 'flowing and flowing and flowing and won't stop. I'm bear-hugging Mick on the board, because his body keeps slipping off, and I'm kicking and Scott is pushing from behind. We were trying to get over to the breakers to get a wave in, but it just wouldn't let us over there. We were in this vortex. We couldn't go outside and around because the waves were so big. We ended up just kicking against the rip for twenty-five minutes.'

About fifteen minutes into their paddling frenzy, Mick came to. He was babbling, making little sense, and Tahlija felt certain he had brain damage. She and Scott continued to urge each other on.

'We're just screaming at each other, "Keep going!" We were both so rooted, we were so buggered.'

At some point the ocean yielded: 'It let us in,' says Tahlija, 'it let us through.' Miraculously, with legs like jelly, they carried Mick onto the beach and collapsed. Tahlija continued to massage the water out of Mick, which now came in rushes, while a bystander called for an ambulance.

Mick was in a coma for four days following the incident. He had a mark across his temple where the doctors believe his board hit him and knocked him out, and evidence of a blow to the back of his head. When he regained consciousness, Mick had a big blank spot in his memory. But before Tahlija had a chance to recount the event, he began telling her of a dream he'd had.

'In the dream, I left my body. I came out of my body and I was looking down at this scenario, and this scenario was us,' he says. 'It was like I was a bird looking down. I was lying on a surfboard and Tahlija was lying over me, and there was this other bloke there. I could see everything as plain as day. I thought she was in trouble. I thought to myself, I've got to get back down there and help her.'

Mick sketched the scene for Tahlija exactly as it had occurred. He described the bend in the wall where they had been struggling, the moment before he came to.

'How do you explain the dream you had?' I ask.

'This is what I feel,' he tells me. 'I believe my spirit was drawing back, and I was on death's door, but something inside me made me fight, and go back in and have another go. I believe my spirit did come back into my body at that moment and kickstart me for another round.'

The point of transition between life and death is a mysterious one. In many ancient traditions, the entrance to the underworld was located beyond a river or body of water. Water, then, provides that transitional point between the mortal and immortal worlds— it is the passage along which the soul must travel on its final spiritual voyage.[26] Perhaps this is not such an unlikely notion. It makes sense in a way, that in our passage beyond the known world we might pass through water, that unknown and unknowable entity.

While thankfully Mick Campbell managed a U-turn at some point along that transitional journey, round two was a slow and steady reawakening. It took him a long time to get his strength back. After coming out of the coma, he had to learn to walk again. It took three months for Mick to venture into the water.

'It's like it zapped the life out of you,' says Tahlija, looking at Mick. 'It zapped your muscle memory.' She turns to me. 'To look at Mick five days before it happened, and then to look at him five days afterwards when he had come out of the coma, it was like the life had been sucked out of his whole body. Everything was so much skinnier. It was wild. His legs, everything. His face was sunken.'

Mick and Tahlija's minds now return to a moment at Lismore Base Hospital, when Mick caught his own reflection in the bathroom mirror for the first time since the accident.

'You were standing holding onto the sink,' says Tahlija, 'because you were so weak and wobbly, and I was standing there next to you holding you up. You said, "That's not me." You said, "That's not me, is it?"'

What an uncanny sensation, I think, to wake up and find that you no longer recognise yourself.

'My eyes were black,' adds Mick. 'I looked into my eyes in the mirror, and it just wasn't me looking back. It was eerie. I was looking at my reflection, and it was like there was no life in it, or very little life. What I was looking at was someone who was very scared. Even I could see I'd been drained. I'd been physically and spiritually drained.'

'How did the experience change you?' I ask.

'I am so different to the person I was. It's ridiculous. It's like I've been given another chance at this whole thing called life. It's made me really appreciate everything so much more.'

These days Mick and Tahlija are ultra-fit, clean-living people.

'Before the Iluka incident I was sober for about three months,' says Mick. 'And I've been sober ever since. It changed a lot of things for me. It switched something inside my head. Because I nearly died, I woke up from the whole thing and went, Far out, I'm still here. I shouldn't be here but I'm still here. It was like I had won the lottery! It was almost like I came out of the coma a new person, and I wanted to celebrate that by being clean and living each day to the max. When I came out of the coma I was like, Fuck this, I'm not drinking, I'm only going to put good food in my body, and I'm going to be the best 2.0 version I can be of myself. The mortality is what's driving me. It made me a way better version of myself, I feel.'

In Winton's novels, Ashcroft says, 'water takes you to the edge of death. It lets you through to that apparent boundary and you go there for the sole purpose of returning. The return is resurrection, rebirth: the return to life gives life meaning'.[27]

We see this recognition of the miracle of life take place in a number of Winton's characters after an extraordinary encounter with the sea. In *Shallows*, Daniel Coupar survives a near-drowning and '[i]n a state akin to hysteria or religious ecstasy', he swims the mile to shore and comes up at Middle Beach 'full of seawater and a curious light'.[28]

Indeed, Mick Campbell went to that apparent boundary and returned, and I can't say whether he had it in him all along, but there is certainly a vitality that bubbles within him now.

But Mick's experience is unique in another sense, too. 'What did you think when you woke up and were told your sweetheart saved your life?' I ask.

'Well for a start it didn't surprise me one bit. Because look at her! She's a specimen.' Mick motions proudly towards Tahlija. 'She's so strong, but more importantly she just knows the water. She's such a water baby you know. She always has been. It didn't surprise me one bit to tell you the truth. And to be honest, I don't think anyone else could have done it, you know what I mean?'

I'm thinking of Michael Adams' meditation on liminality,

about our connections, through water, to those myths of 'mermen and mermaids: beings between human and water creature.'

While Tahlija agrees she had a lot to do with keeping Mick alive that day, she insists that there were other forces at work too. Scott's assistance was invaluable, while the big-wave leggie that Mick had put on at the last minute was a vital lifeline in keeping him connected to his surfboard, and therefore discoverable in the maelstrom of moving water. But there was something else at play, suggests Tahlija, something bigger and less tangible.

'We were just paddling and paddling and paddling, and we'd be so close, and then another surge would come and we'd be back where we started. But something happened in the water that day that I can't describe. Something was watching over us. I'm not sure if it was the ancestors, but something helped us get back to shore that day because we weren't getting back there. We were struggling for so long, we were so tired, and then it was like something lifted us and took us in. We were stuck in this rip, and then it was like the ocean just let us in. Like, I'm going to teach you a lesson, and then I'm going to let you in. You've seen how powerful I am, you've seen all my different faces, and now I'm going to let you in and let you off this one.'

I want to know how it changed her relationship with the sea, which, it seems to me, had always been a trusted friend.

'I've never been afraid of the sea, but this made me afraid,' she admits. 'It made me very afraid for a long time. Just to see how small I was that day on that wall, and to see how little power I had over the sea. It made me realise how much respect she deserves—the ocean—and that anything at any split second could go wrong out there. And I suppose as a kid I never once thought about that. I guess in some sense there was no respect there. And that was my learning out of the whole experience.'

These days Tahlija is on constant watch when she's in the water. She's learned to be less self-centred in a line-up—something that many of us surfers are guilty of. If she sees someone take off on a heavy one, she'll always wait to see if they come up on the other side.

'And I always freak out, still to this day, when someone doesn't come up. I reckon I could count ten people I've paddled over to, thinking that they're drowning. I still do it. I did it at Town Beach the other day.'

It has taken both Mick and Tahlija a long time to regain their confidence in heavy waves. Just like the ocean swimmers and the sailors, they returned to the scene of their trauma. A year after the accident, the couple drove north to Iluka breakwall.

'It was one to two foot, clean and beautiful, perfect wedges off the wall.'

'How did you feel being back there?'

'It was pretty weird paddling out against the wall,' says Tahlija.

'It was closure,' adds Mick thoughtfully. 'To have that sense of peacefulness, like the ocean was inviting us back. It was something that needed to happen.'

Since then, Mick and Tahlija have gradually worked their way back up to chasing the kinds of waves they did pre-2017. In 2019 they travelled across the country, surfing some heavy slabs on the far-flung South Australian coast, before they veered north to meet a swell at Gnaraloo. On this trip they once again found their groove, and that return to self, that recognition, was incredibly gratifying. But before long Mick was sidelined with a dislocated shoulder, and later, Tahlija with a torn ACL. They laugh about these small setbacks, which have little weight in comparison to what they encountered at Iluka. They're both back in the water now, and preparing their troopie for another trip to the bottom end. When you've known that infinity feeling that Tahlija described earlier, I suppose there's no other option. I remember the way their eyes twinkled as they described it. I expect that these two will continue to move through life at the jagged edge of things, defying reason, making the unmakeable.

On that calm and serene weekend morning, as I surf at Iluka breakwall, I'm filled with a mixture of emotions. The smooth, silky water restores and enlivens, and yet the knowledge of what has happened here—of Mick and Tahlija's experience—is never far from my mind. Even so, I welcome the playful touches of the sea against my skin, the anticipation of an oncoming set, the exhilarating rush of the drop and the freedom of the dance as I career along the face of my final wave. I emerge from the water, like the ocean swimmers, renewed, reminded yet again of the holiness of the world. I stand on the shoreline pacified, like Tony Mowbray might be, as he stands in the cockpit, hands on the wheel, overlooking the endless stretch of blue. I think it must be this feeling that keeps people returning, time and again, to the sea. I take one final glance at the wide expanse, with Tahlija's dreaded breakwall unfolding like a staircase to that arcane place beyond. Like most people who devote themselves to the wilds, the seafarers I met with—the swimmers, the sailor and the surfers—have all encountered its wrath in various ways. They have been enraptured, humbled, transformed, each returning with a new perspective on their own small place within that great wash of ocean, and yet all of them unwilling to plant their feet permanently on land. The mystery of the ocean intrigues and invites; like the murky depths of a book as complex and multifaceted as Homer's *Odyssey* or Melville's *Moby Dick*, it keeps you returning to its many pages, knowing you may never understand it completely. And perhaps this is the truth of all significant friendships.

A Man Above the Reef
Jake Sandtner

Based on true events

Beginning

Well let's see if Taj can get himself out of combination here. He tucks in, finds the barrel, gets the exit. Driving out onto the open face now, smooth, but he needs something high impact … and … he takes a fall before getting to the end section.
—Ronnie Blakey, Round One, Heat Ten: Fiji Pro 2016[1]

The Free Surfer

Yallingup, Australia

Taj has accomplished much. He's thirty-eight. A newspaper lies open on the counter but, since he's nursing a one-year-old, he turns the pages of a cardboard picture book.

'The cow jumped over the moon,' he reads.

It's morning. He's scheduled for Fiji. Taj's little family join him at the breakfast counter. His home is white-walled, recently reno'd and (despite Bec's eye for interior decoration) littered with knitted dolls, bub bibs and paraphernalia off the changing table.

Music plays in the background, a melody pleasing both Arabella and Bec. Bec swings her hips in the kitchen. Arabella stomps on his lap. Taj is amused at their mismatched rhythm.

At the terminal, Taj kisses his family goodbye. Recalls tender moments. He's been in the nest, mostly, in his circular dream home (it took offer after offer to acquire) and thinks about when he'll next be back. Tries to concentrate less on the shake of his fingers and more on anything but. Now his career's catching up with him ... Shit, isn't that a thought?

How else d'you dodge nerves? Nostalgia's a drug in itself. Though perhaps this type of recollection ain't helpful, for it's surely bringing on the nerves twofold. He sweats, in an airport of all places, boarding a plane to infinity, remembering the beginning of it all.

Taj remembers his time off tour, his surfing that was free. *Sabotaj*, the film, hijacked this offshoot of his career way back. Billabong pitched a profile concept to him. He was nineteen, and, with Jack McCoy leading the production, it was an exciting opportunity to showcase his young self to the world. Not to mention to get his hands on a bit of coin.

McCoy knew Taj prior to the making of *Sabotaj*. He had spent time in Western Australia and was familiar with the breaks of Busselton. The film's combo production featured both home footage and original content, and Taj's first taste of free surfing earned *Sabotaj* a reputation as one of the best profile surf films produced. With revolutionary airs, a showcase of Perth-side barrels, and an insight into Australia's newest circuit tour edition, *Sabotaj* was the key that unlocked Taj's love for surfing beyond scorecards. His father's creative flair as an elegant surfer and dexterous musician began to come out in Taj as he explored the flipside of surf, the artistic recording of it. It's inexplicable, the love he has for film production and editing processes. Standing in the booth on his second profile film, *Montaj*, he couldn't resist selecting tracks, cropping frames and syncing playful nonsense into what would become another acclaimed feature. *Montaj* was a well-needed creative outlet. Curated by Taj, his old man Vance and others including McCoy, it was a film worth drooling over. Being his favourite of the two -*taj* movies, he was stoked when the profile flick unexpectedly won a handful of prestigious awards, including *Surfer Magazine*'s Movie of the Year. The trophy on the shelf a lure, Taj's fascination with the free surfing world was recast.

Competing on tour, Taj stretched himself thin between surfing worlds. In 2003, *Stab Magazine* founder and editor Sam McIntosh approached Taj with an idea.

'I have this book in my head,' Sam said.

'Yeah? What is it? Alright, let's do it,' said Taj.

Taj Burrow's Book of Hot Surfing was published as a gag/credible book of surfing photos, anecdotes and hot tips for surfers. Taj can barely believe the number of books he continues to sign at events, with groms and adults alike bringing the book in as if it's a prized classic.

Taj's next film project was *Fair Bits!*

Filmed in California, the collection of short films was uncharted territory, famed for its experimental mix of wicked surfing, innovative behind-the-scenes footage, skits and never-attempted filming techniques such as heli-frames. In conception, it had an appeal that drew the involvement of Andy Irons and Ben Stiller, hungry as crocs to sunbathing tourists. *Fair Bits!* had a fragrance that stirred the otherwise stale air of surf films. When Taj began rolling the camera, he felt the pull.

The flair in *Fair Bits!* unleashed creativity in Taj's surfing. The surf world lived for creative moments like a tradie waited on smoko. Taj felt deep down that he had to include the normal stuff—the surfing everyone knew and loved, the angles that screamed modern professionalism—but that, he knew, was also commercialism sucking the life out of the free.

'What else is there to do?' the crew asked.

'We could film from a helicopter,' Taj said. 'We could get angles on surfing that no-one has ever shot before.'

Hiring Joe Driver, an ex-Vietnam heli-pilot, wasn't cheap, but it was coin well spent.

Joe followed Taj around the swells of California, banking and dipping. The man could fly. Taj dominated the line-up, full or empty. The waves were average height, clean, the kind that allowed for speed, flight and exaggerated turns. Taj exercised aerials and the earth would shake. When the waves grew, so did his tenacity. He had blokes out there with him on jetskis, towing him onto the larger sets. All the while, a helicopter the size of a small bus chased him inches from the water's surface, camera crew hanging out the open door like howler monkeys. It was the time of revolution.

It wasn't the only time helicopters would appear in Taj's free-surfing career. After *Fair Bits!*, there came the attempted acid drop—not that kind, but the kind that buckled you hard enough to rip an arm from its socket. In an event covered by *Stab Magazine*, Taj, with a couple of mates, attempted the world's first acid drop, but to no avail; only memories and a crippled interview with the mag to show for it.

'What led you to jump from the chopper?' *Stab* asked.

'I just like the idea of trying something that no-one's ever tried before, and I really wanted to know if it was possible. We had all the ingredients, it's just the chopper pilot needed to be a little bit more cluey on how swells work.'

Taj knew this wouldn't have happened if he'd had Joe flying. When *Stab* asked about the likelihood of landing one with the pilot who flew for *Fair Bits!* he replied, nonchalant, 'I reckon we would have stuck one, for sure.'

In the months that followed the helicopter diving, Taj's belly began to fall over his size thirty-three boardshorts and something in him snapped. He was twenty-seven now and at the crossroads of his career: he knew he'd never give up on free surfing but if he wanted to chase down the crown, his days were numbered. He hated being torn between two worlds, and though he preferred not to change anything, he made a decision: his next focus would be the ASP Championship Tour. Believing he could maintain a higher ranking on tour if he focussed on competitive surfing rather than free surfing, he knuckled down and got right to it.

And here he is, getting right to it. Final boarding call for Nadi. Eleven years ago, he'd fearlessly jumped out of a helicopter onto a six-foot set. Now he's stepping onto a plane shit-scared of coming last at the Fiji Pro, his last ever event on tour.

Round One

Cloudbreak, Fiji

In the wake of his retirement announcement, Taj finds himself sweating in the cool waters of Fiji's Cloudbreak line-up. Boats rock over the reef, one bearing the red flag that indicates the loss of time. His trusted, yet discoloured, surfboard keeps Taj afloat while the wind tears at his white jersey like a cutlass. Taj doesn't know how he'll fare but the attention is contributing to his anxiety. He can feel eyes from the charter boats burning holes in the back of his head, and millions more through the lenses of livestreamed cameras. Already he's allowed his underlying clumsiness—which he knows, in a way, is the foundational part of him—to take centre stage, and while the sun melts the zinc under his eyes, and salt numbs the inside of his nose, Taj Burrow releases a long-held breath, contemplating the end. For though this is only the beginning of the round, it can now be regarded as the final commencement.

One of those heats, he sighs. Do I have a shot here? Just one more wave. So he goes. As the northerly gale blankets the sky with greying clouds, the sun shoots streamers of light across distant Tavarua Island that dance on the water's clear surface and dazzle the pockets of coral and rocks on the reef below. Taj's scooped hands drag him onward, hunting atop the reef, hunting the line-up, for something not there.

Taj pictures it. A left rolling in, hollow and relentless, firing over the reef, spitting as the wind flies from its back. Gliding across the water at breakneck speed, dragging his hand across the belly of the tube. He imagines this, yes, it will come … Isn't there a universal dream for such waves?

No such waves are rolling through and Taj has ... shit. The clock unwinds; 1:59 remains.

Submerged to the hip in the ocean, far enough away to be a shape to the people on the boats but close enough as to be broadcasted in high definition across the globe, Taj paddles toward the inside of the break, dodging looks from the competition with a determined frown. He's left his nest atop an angled hill in Yallingup, sheer as the cliff face it is perched upon, and his partner Rebecca, yet to wear a diamond ring, and little Arabella.

He feels their presence; or is this some instinctual placebo fatherhood has gifted him? Who does he have to thank for his luxurious lifestyle? This, probably, he thinks, acknowledging the circus set-up around him in paradise. The World Surf League is anything but subtle with its raucous event bump-ins. It's a game, after all. Taj took little time to consider whether he agreed or disagreed with their practice when he signed up for the game, years ago. With all their bells and whistles, the WSL's encampment in the Fiji Isles is perhaps one of the things he loves most, not to mention his long-time source of income.

He shakes his head, ridding himself of the white noise as he passes Adrian Buchan, blond hair swept back over his forehead, and even in the heat of the frying pan Taj recognises the shadow of a smile on the face of the New South Welshman; even if it's a figment of his imagination, he twigs Ace could conjure one at any moment, and it'll knock everyone dead. Impossible not to like the man. Ace sitting with his chest above water, the reef deep enough below him to be a foggy illusion, bobbing in the moment, looking into the distance like a dingo with game in the air, nothing but the line-up in his thoughts. But Ace is in the wrong spot. Taj clears his throat and continues paddling across the line-up, stroke after stroke, getting to where he needs to be. If anything, the paddling is the remedy he seeks. The lactic acid building in his chest, shoulders, back, after battling the tides for half an hour, gives him a focus, a way out of his own head, a way to ignore the adversity of the cameras. Ace may have the leg-up but he ain't Taj, and Taj can feel it. Fiji is his. Head cleared, he stops, sits atop his board and feels the tides drag, gentle, against the bottom of his feet. He smiles.

The horizon bleeds with the glare of the sun, the multitude of small boats rock over the reef. Are the people in them pointing at him? Somewhere beyond their heads he knows there is Tavarua and Namotu. Perhaps he can see the further island's white sand, or is that just the glare? The winding path from Yallingup has ended with paranoia, it seems, luring him to focus more on the glaze before his eyes than the next wave. Then he feels the tide shift, the solid drift, something is coming ...

He still has a shot. He's in the section, is he not? The waves have fallen miserably thus far, but now as the clock winds down Taj finds the irony in the turn of the tides. Glancing over at the flash of a red jersey paddling furiously in his wake, he sees the chop has calmed and Jordy Smith, the large South African, is hustling—throwing his priority in Taj's face as if being free of having to break combination isn't enough. How could he have forgotten his second round-one combatant?

Taj—who knows he should be staying out of his own head—welcomes the distraction as Jordy rocks on his board and trains the nose of his stick like a drawn arrow, and the first of many somethings-to-come comes. Jordy has eyes only for it. Down the line, Taj spies Ace, not deep enough to be in a comfortable spot though paddling keener than Taj feels.

It has to be Adrian and Jordy. Are there two nicer blokes than these in the world?

What's happening? Are these truly his thoughts? Now? In the fire of the sea, the deep of the reef, the final row of the round?

And then Jordy's upon him. And then he's gone.

The roar of the hollow tube cuts across the reef and Taj watches its back as it screams against the wind. This is warfare and Jordy is dicing Ace and him like new recruits. Aren't I the vet here? The back of Jordy's board tears through the wave, spraying white foam into the air with a vigorous slash. The wind drops spray onto Taj's face.

A sloppy floater and head-dipped barrel ain't getting me through, Taj thinks, wiping his face clean.

It's the biggest set of the heat and the Fijian gods rumble with laughter—or is that just another South African hack? Taj thrusts the nose of his board into the nook of his chest and begins the final paddle. The water begins to gush him, his chest close to the board, head tilted forward: heaving with every stroke, Taj allows the water to right him. Nerves fade though anxiety's pitched in his shoulders, riding him as easily as he rides his own waxed Mayhem deck.

He stands.

Instinct takes the reins, guides his nimble stance to a crouch. Grabbing the thin rails of his compressed board, Taj feels the fins take purchase as the strength of Cloudbreak's jaw sucks open. The wave's hot breath is of a beast when it spits onto his back; the roaring spiral envelops him inside a four-foot tube. Stilled, he maintains speed as he's sucked back, down the throat of the barrel. The wave is moving fast, racing across the reef, inhaling the shallows and everything in between. The lips of the wave creep further from Taj's outstretched fingers as he is swallowed.

He banks into the face, hoping to generate momentum, the flash of the rocks beneath his feet a crude reminder of the price of being eaten. Taj leans into the exit and shoots from the wave's closing curtain with an angry blast of spray as a parting gift.

The force of the blow throws him. Unbalanced, sweating, arms stiff as he skates an invisible beam, Taj hears a familiar ring. The face of the wave staggers as he peers down the line, closes on him as he focuses on that ring; the lip quivers. Bumps appear, impossibly, to break beneath his feet. His stomach slaps with the surface of water when he falls. The final blows of the horn fade on the air, the hooter sounds and the heat, inevitably, closes as the ocean swallows him whole.

Shit, he thinks, straining against the stress of his lungs, I've come fucking last.

TB: Yeah, everyone's just paying more attention, and I do feel a bit weird. I don't like that sort of attention personally. So I was a bit spooked in that way but I was just thinking, 'I'm going to go in and enjoy myself, I'm going to drink beers and I'm going to just pick my moments to party and my moments to be disciplined and to put on the performance I really want to.' So, yeah, I went in prepared and trying to be as relaxed as I could. Enjoyed some beers and my mateship with everyone. And then really, you know, surf good as well. I was just trying to balance it.[2]

Some paths, once set upon, give no other option but to paddle on, while others offer a bank of reprieve. Taj, paddling toward the boats, peering at the depths beneath, contemplates his loss and finds himself at last pondering the possibility of changing the well-worn path he has trodden for decades. His competitive surfing career is ending and the exit signs to the unknown are beginning to flash with warning. What waits is a mystery; however, the realisation dawns that no matter the outcome of Fiji, he'll be leading this new life soon enough. And there is no way he's letting his last memory of surfing on tour become a repeat of what has just happened here.

The boats, brimming with local charter drivers and fellow competitors, bob in Taj's wake and lift his mood. He passes his board to a local man, who carefully lowers it to the deck, and Taj climbs aboard. The boats make a pointed job of drifting at least two metres from each other, as if separated by invisible blocks, and it burns Taj; it burns so hard it becomes obvious. The boat he's boarded contains no stoked faces.

Cloudbreak roars at his back, and the grim expressions worn by his comrades speak volumes. Taj has sat a mediocre heat with mediocre waves only to be robbed by the seas. The swell is surging and heat eleven, the next heat, is graced with pulse.

Taj sighs. Let them think this is the end. Most speculation is born of deceit, or ego, and Taj Burrow has learned to be but a feather in the wind over his twenty years on the circuit. Let them rumour over my slumped shoulders, let them laugh into their hands. I'm still here for another round; watch out whoever's drawn.

Taj swipes a crinkled palm over the shaved left side of his mohawked head. He's comforted by his own determination, and if he were to look up from his salt-stained hands and forget about ripping the jersey from his chest, he'd see the encouraging glances, the idolatry from the local groms, the endearment from those he has just surfed against. He'd notice this, and ignore the attention that's on him from the outlets such as WSL, *Tracks*, *Surfing World*, *Surfing Life*, *Monster Children*. They go on. Who isn't talking about Taj Burrow's retirement? Speculation is the enemy of truth.

Contrary to what he knows, or what he thinks he knows, Taj is giving them the show they so desperately deserve. He'll hold tight to his integrity the only way he knows how—by surfing.

Truth is, he's not even here to win the thing anymore.

He's here in Fiji on tour for the last time, and he ain't chasing a victory. It feels strange to contemplate. He's here to surf.

Find the right exit.

So … surf, Taj Burrow. Surf like the world's watching.

Because it is.

Namotu

Namotu, Fiji

He wakes in his bed—a simple sheet, a single mattress, mosquito net drawn—totally and utterly alone. Taj has forgotten to charge his phone, not that it really matters this far from the mainland, so he sits up, the palms of his hands rest neatly on the skirt of his mattress, his feet find the cool tiles. His head aches slightly; too much going on there.

Taj's room, the bunker, is closed to the rising sun by thin, white cotton curtains that hang over a set of double doors leading to a small balcony. The walk is slow. He draws the curtains back and opens the doors. Immersed in the sun's early light, the smell of Fiji welcomes him. The world rights itself again. The mainland songbirds are absent here; in their place is the gentle rock of the tides lapping on the shore. It's as if the ocean is breathing.

In. Out.

On mainland Fiji, with every exhalation the ocean pushes the muck from its belly onto the sand. Fiji is third world. Uninsulated homes on wavering stilts, chipped fluorescent paint and the contents a questionable balance between hygienic and functional. The gardens are garnished with weeds. But above all this the sun shines and the air is clean. The children play, and grandfathers sing. The mothers dance, and the food on the table is organic. The smiles on the faces are real.

Humankind cannot be stopped, its instinct is to evolve, and that's a thought that strikes all too firmly with Taj, and many other surfers, no matter their origin. The ocean is his livelihood, his passion, his career, and year by year, week by week, humans and their industries threaten its very existence. In the future perhaps there'll be events dedicated solely to saving the ocean, or raising awareness of the fact at least. Only time will tell.

Taj leans on the railing of his balcony, his mind wanders. The mainland's far behind him, sitting square in the east with its hotels and tourist pockets and polluted beaches, but this ... this is Fiji. Fine, white-grained sands free from swamp, tall palm trees with coconuts ripe for the taking, salt on the tongue, in the air, and the shore decorated with nothing but shells and debris from lonely coral castaways. The water is blue here, clear as a pane of glass placed on lazy sand, and at night the stars number in the thousands.

No plastic. No nappies, loose-leaf paper, straws, cups or plastic bags. None of that out here and it's a miracle that such islands can so remain in this era.

I'm in paradise right now for my last event on tour, are you kidding?

Back in his room the small fan creaks as it turns. Taj grabs a crumpled towel from the couch and heads out. Already in his Billabong Tribongs, black with a two-toned twill of floral greys, a size too big so his arse crack catches the breeze, he sets out onto the cold morning sand. Who knows what the time is, and who needs to know? Sure, it's winter back home but are seasonal laws acknowledged out here in the South Pacific archipelagos?

The sand grain is thicker than home, thicker than the golden beaches of the Yallingup coast. It sticks to his feet even though they aren't wet, and the colour is a wish-wash of dark browns through golden through white. There are shells and large, smooth stones, driftwood and coral cones. Taj touches and studies a few of them as he descends to the lapping shore.

Suddenly, the clack of sticks. Taj turns toward the morning sun, toward a man perched on a boulder. The man has short hair, buzzed thin with lines running parallel, streaking through to the skin, shining against the horizon. Taj knows him, vaguely. He's the one who greeted them all a couple of days back with the *bula* ceremony. He's also the one, Taj remembers, who served behind the bar last night, makes a mean pina colada. Wasn't he part of the procession party too?

Taj pictures it: he steps off the boat onto Namotu proper, where the locals have a different tradition, different view of respect. Back in Australia, it's all firm handshakes, posture and eye contact, but here ... here they keep their seat and look up at you towering above. They clap their hands together rather than squeeze yours and for some reason it feels genuine all the same.

Now the man is waving a giant hand over his head as Taj nears the shore, his grin splitting his face and those huge white teeth make the smile infectious. Once Taj believed such greetings were because he was partly famous ... well, there are a lot of pro surfers here. But come to Fiji even once, and you'll know it has nothing to do with who you are. That's the truth of the matter; it's because Fijians are just so happy to be.

Taj bids good morning with an outstretched arm. The kind that looks as though he's grabbing for something with spread fingers. The man, in kind, strikes the stick in his left hand back down onto the stick in his right, letting loose another loud clack that the entire island can hear, for sure. What is it? Taj wonders. A blessing? A song?

His toes touch the water and suddenly he's sinking to his ankles in the shallows. The warmth rides higher up his legs and the goosebumps of the early morning die as he rocks his elbows back with a final step before diving. The tropical waters of Namotu consume him, wash him, and after a stroke he opens his eyes. The reward is a crystalline blue landscape. He comes up for air and dives back underneath like a porpoise, like he's of the ocean, as if he's meant to be here. And when he comes up for air a second time and stands waist-deep, staring off at the distant reef, peering into Cloudbreak's den, he wonders, just wonders in silence, What's gonna happen next?

TB: *I prepared particularly well because I wanted to go out swinging, I wanted to put in a good performance. I didn't have in my head, 'Oh, I've got to fucking win Fiji, it's my last hurrah' kinda thing. I just wanted to go there and surf well, you know? I just wanted to put on a good show, no matter what. In preparation for that I made sure my boards were dialled, may have done a bit of extra training and stretching and I just went there to enjoy the moment. I chose Fiji because that has got to be one of my favourites—it's got to be my favourite. Not only is it the sickest venue with the sickest waves and you're on this perfect, beautiful island with a bunch of mates—and you're all just having a sick time and it doesn't feel like a contest—not only that but I just love it.*

Round Two

Cloudbreak, Fiji

Taj runs a hand along the nose of his board, tiny fibreglass specks come loose in the water. He's tracing small compressions with the rough edge of a fingernail, picking at stray wax clumps. The Billabong sticker is old and tattered, barely holding on to the deck. The black outline shimmers beneath the surface of the tide, where the glare sheens. Glowing like the pulse throbbing in his wrists, the board is as much a part of him as his own legs. This board is his favourite of the quiver, and he strokes the nose unconsciously.

Taj isn't one to get rid of boards he loves. He clings to sentimentality, of a sort. He wonders why you'd get rid of boards at all, especially those you've done stuff on. Like drop out of a helicopter with. Perhaps boards are just equipment to some surfers, like a ratty pair of boots for a hiker or a racquet that's hit too many balls for a tennis player. He wonders about surfers, how they surf for the chase, the chase of feeling, the chase of the next wave. He wonders whether others on tour, like him, hold onto memories like he does boards. Maybe others think coin is enough, in the end.

Does legacy mean anything?

Days like today are full of sentimentality, almost ritualistic— and because of this path, the path we all must take, unknown, and aptly named The Future, Taj feels he needs to control as much as he can right now, and his 5'11" Mayhem hasn't really let him down lately; except for the fucking compressions beneath his fingertips, where did these come from?

Pushing away chunks of driftwood caught in the foamy discharge from a charter boat, he carefully measures his section by regarding the sponsor tower, a jutting beacon over the reef. Not only is the multistorey complex a perfect canvas to slap a Samsung Galaxy logo on, it also houses the judging panel, and the production studio and the cameras that will follow his every move.

The islands are a dreamy backdrop of green hills, white sand and dense palm jungles, and it's funny how not many are blinking twice at it; all eyes are on the horizon, staring into the endless blue as if it's the only colour in the world.

He resumes eyeing his spot, and ten paddles or so later the water feels cooler, as if the reef has dropped from beneath him to reveal a gaping jaw of deep nothingness. He takes this as an omen for no other reason than because. The heat has only just begun and here he is already packing his suitcase. Sure as all shit he's afraid of losing again, that's what a couple of days of stressing can do to a man.

Still working his section, letting baggage drip from his palms with every drift-defying stroke, he pauses. Searching across the shoulders of lulling sets. Minutes have sailed. Not a single wave to his name. Yet. He's got this idea of quality versus quantity rambling in the walls of his head, a tactic that's either gonna send him unhypothetically packing, or save his sorry arse.

A lone figure in a tight red jersey sits atop his board facing west. Caio Ibelli, his hands gripping his board's rails, his jaw working hard at chewing the inside of his cheek as he studies the horizon like everybody else. He glances over at Taj, as turgid waters ripple, telling of incoming lines. The frock of the water laps over the edges of Taj's board. Of the sounds he's heard, the gentle knock of water on fibreglassed foam is one he'll cherish until they bury him. A hollow knock that boardriders the world over can relate to, the anchor of them all, a soft sound both tranquil and exhilarating. Taj swishes the water around his palms and resonates with the soft thunk as the sea traces the planed surface of his board.

Taj moves to within a couple of lengths of Caio and sits back. Caio's a fresh face on tour. One of his first trips to Fiji; it's obvious in how he fidgets, paddling back and forth across the line-up, rocking like Arabella does on her wooden horse. Taj doesn't strike him out, he's still a threat; every damn surfer on tour is. Plus, he'd be lying if he didn't admit to Caio's one-of-the-better-rookies status. But experience is weighing the scales. Cloudbreak's got to be one of Taj's favourite spots, he knows these waters, and they him.

He isn't worried. Besides, this one looks alright. Caio notices it too, gives him a look.

Taj has priority, swings his board round with a knowing smile.

The waves are better. They aren't freight-training but they're four-foot and spewing their guts up thanks to the high tide. The wind's dropped so the spray just kind of lingers as waves barrel by, rains down with the force of a sneeze's spittle, but best of all is how long the face stretches on these things. Long, crumbly glass mounds, a Fiji recipe for deep, drivey turns.

Easy to get speed and even easier to hack. Good but not great Cloudbreak. A sure second if he had to score it, and now Taj is steaming to have another crack. He rocks his weight into the paddle, chest pressing forward, kicking as the wave grabs and throws him with a punctual follow-through.

He stands, presses upright and primes the drop, no rail grabs, no bogging, no clumsy take-offs today, thanks. The wave opens. Throwing down the line, racing, pumping, stomping his feet, leaning down the stretch. Throwing his front foot to the right, he lets the momentum take him as he drops to meet the point where flat water and wave churn, and thrusts his weight into the turn, heading back for the peak. The white wall is crumbling, no barrels, but setting him up for a lengthy ride. Crisp, smooth.

Same as the first turn. So's the next.

Taj smacks the lip, fins just shy from cutting through the peak.

He doesn't hesitate; rocking with all his speed he throws back down for another long drive, the foam slices up and over the rails and leaves a trail of gutted foam in his wake—like lines traced in sand. He shifts his weight again, attacking the wave's head over and over again. Taj's own head is as clear as it's ever been, there's nothing but the next turn, and he reads the wave as if it's already written. Each snap's an improvement Taj is drafting as he carves his story into the wave in a language all his own.

A long carve draws out each centimetre. His board's a part of him, an extension of his will, this is where he belongs. He shifts for a final charge through the bumpy end section. Eyes only for the lip—he hits with a slash, a goodnight kiss as the face loses volume. Buckets scream off the back of the wave.

Taj lands with bent knees, turns off the back, diving onto his stomach, tiny droplets fall as he paddles over the reef, eyeing the way forward, lining up the Samsung Galaxy tower again.

You see that?

He bails from a crumbler that's wont to dog him judging by the way foam leaks across the face. One such ride would make for a bumpy, low-scoring time. Taj gives the wave nothing, not even a glance, it isn't even worth the paddle. Opting for the immediate fade, he doesn't attempt a turn. The judges still score him a 0.7, which is more than it deserves.

Above railings of fibreglass charter boats, a heap of eskies lie ignored, wrapped in towels and brimming with beers. Heads bob, intent on the bout. The long, littered row of skis is rigged, harnessed by anchors and joined at the bows to boats beside them, restricting unlearned seamen from floating off. The reef loves a feed. Besides the other athletes, the boats keep afloat faces that no-one at home cares to know but in truth these people are the backbone of most tour contests. Medics, managers, trainers, physios, journos, mates—all that. One fella holds a flag, flapping it like a two-year-old on cordial. The number 99 sings proud.

The sun cuts a hole in the eastern sky, golden and bright and near impossible to ignore. Soon the tan lines will appear like unwanted tattoos. Unless you're rolling it on with a paintbrush, sunscreen'll do fuck-all in a place like this.

Taj paddles between the chops on the water, exchanges the occasional glance with Caio who moves hastily on to deeper water with an air of confidence. Taj's two-wave combination score hasn't gotten him over the line, he needs to pull a seven-something outta the bag yet; Caio has caught almost triple the number of waves Taj has even contemplated.

Beneath the water's surface there's nothing but coloured reef—stark white, emerald green, tree-bark brown—future scars.

Taj reins in. Facing north with the nose of his arrow tucked beneath the surface and comfortable between his clamped legs, he fidgets with the water's top, waiting. Seven minutes remain. Even with priority he's nervous about his quality tactic. He has passed on a few that might've just given him the edge, or the confidence.

Anything but last, a voice whispers.

He paddles toward a roll on the horizon.

From the tower's vantage, Taj is seen ignoring the pointed job spectators are doing, cheering and hoo-harring as they lean on the boat railings just to get a glimpse of him. He paddles for what will be his highest scoring wave of the day.

It's bigger than the last, a nice five-footer—the kind that comes through on the rare set, hitting the reef–sand combo just right. Taj feels the rush of wind as he's picked up in the wave's torment, the gush of churning water, the reflection of the hot sun on the sharp reef, and he's thrown downward, his board skidding across the surface of the glassy body.

One second.

Three.

He shoots to his feet.

At first he looks sketchy, like he's nervous, his knees bobble, clack together, his arms outthrust in a sort of gotta-keep-my-balance regime. But all this lasts just a moment; if the commentary box hadn't mentioned it the world mightn't have noticed. It's a classic set-up turn, a tender slash across the water's top, not too deep, but enough to manoeuvre as the wave forms.

The first set-up is followed by something a little harder but not quite the quintessential move of the heat. It's a beautiful wave, hulking, throwing a shadow across the surface enough to block the sun's glare, and the peak is steep, and best of all, if tamed rightly, it has the potential to earn him high numbers.

The wave is over by the fourth turn but the finale, a backhand snap, is executed with precision, speed, just on the sweet spot. He has a lot of speed to arrive at the lip, enough to send pellets of water shooting for the stars. The judges eat it up, this much spray served with a carve-mastery is what they look for in these sorts of conditions.

Satisfied and somewhat anxious, Taj turns off the wave and calls for the jetski, paddles from the northern section knowing he has enough time for another.

He has to hurry back and squeeze something out of Caio's priority, but what Taj doesn't know is the level of stoke from the judging tent, not to mention the commentary box.

He has scored an 8.03.

Fizzing for more, he jumps on the ski unawares, grips the back of the bloke's shoulder and drops his board by his feet. The ski hurries, but there's an unconscious part of Taj that knows: that's all she wrote for Caio.

He can barely hold back a childish grin. That's how you surf Cloudbreak.

The Gift

Namotu, Fiji

The announcement comes at breakfast. Taj sits alongside Sponnas as he scoffs an omelette, the stench of shrooms and thick-cut capsicum fills his senses. Sponnas is Taj's good mate, has been for close to fifteen years. The blond-haired man nurses a Canon camera on his lap as though it's a baby, his knees tucked up, forced together, bare feet on their balls, so the heavy equipment doesn't slide nowhere. Doesn't stop him from hoeing into his eggs and beans. It'll be a while before they eat in silence like this again, not that Taj notices.

The loss of round one is still eating at him. Mate, it doesn't feel good. That's for sure. Losing the opening round with nerves and jitters shaking him makes him look like a rookie. But a bad heat is a bad heat, and Taj can live with that. What he can't live with, he decides, is silence.

'Mate, I cooked it the other day. Got lucky against Caio,' Taj says.

Sponnas looks over a fork of shaking eggs, the utensil hovering somewhere between his chin and mouth. He shrugs, shovels the eggs between his lips and draws the fork out slow, like Arthur prising Excalibur from the stone. 'You had a fucking bad heat, mate. Get over it.' Sponnas thrusts the four prongs of the fork in Taj's direction. 'You got a few in there, the waves were just too sloppy.'

'Yeah, how's the—what's this old boy doing?' Taj's laugh drives forth like a battering ram. 'It's fucking nine o'clock, mate.'

Gannon is tall and handsome with a prominent jaw, he's also adamant about this eighty:twenty rule. Eighty of the good shit, twenty of the bad shit, in and out of the water that rule applies. But fuck me, it's nine o'clock in the morning! Gannon walks over, gives Mick and Joel a brief wink from across the room and squeezes in beside Taj and Sponnas. He places three Fiji Bitters in the middle of the table, a smile splits his rugged face.

'You're keen,' Sponnas says.

'I was just off talking to the boys and you're not gonna believe it,' Gannon says. 'Cloudbreak's flat as. Barely breaking. It is legit small as all shit. They've just called it. Round three's not kicking, not being reassessed for another week'. Gannon scoops up a Bitter and cracks the top off the sweating bottle.

'So we're stuck here for seven days with an open bar,' Taj says. 'On my retirement.'

Holy shit yes.

Shortly after the lay-days announcement ricochets across the island, Taj sits with his feet on the railing back at his room. He can see the short drop to the sand over the tops of his toes, his mates smash Bitters by his side as if they're water. His feet are black from walking everywhere in bare feet.

The sun is at its zenith, high as the clouds are thin, hot as the waves are flat. It's the smallest he's known Cloudbreak for a tour event, and Taj has been going for a record eighteen years. And yet Taj is a surfer, an optimist and a pessimist, honest but an exaggerator. The waves are flat, unsurfable, a sloppy, incoherent mess. He places an empty bottle of Bitter gently on the table. The sun warms his skin. Gannon and Sponnas bicker.

'You're pissed, ya idiot. Gone. Done. Game over,' Gannon says.

Sponnas cracks the cap off another bottle. Tosses it into the bathroom bin they've dragged from Taj's room, watches the cap sailing in the air, flipping flippantly, heads, tails, heads. Taj grins, head lolling.

'What then?'

'What do you mean, what then? What type of question's that? What do you mean?'

'Farkawff, what should we do then?'

'How should I know? But you're onto something. I'm just not diving in the middle of the ocean with nothing other than a fucking water spear thing, with you lunatics, shooting fish.'

'Or sharks.'

'We'll just go fishing.'

'That's what I said.'

'Without the spears.'

'Why without spears?'

'Well, if we get eaten—'

'Or lost.'

'Or lost. Then Taj can't put Florence in his place.'

'Right. But what does Taj prefer?'

'Eh. Good question. It's his retirement.'

'Kinda like a bachelor party.'

'Then we're the best men.'

'And the best men organise the party.'

'So what do we do?'

'Fishing?'

'Fishing.'

'With spears.'

'No spears.'

'Fine. With beers.'

'Beers. Yes.'

'It's a start. Let's think some more. We got ourselves a starting plan and that's a start.'

'What else you reckon? That's just one day.'

'Let's just start with one day.'

'Alright, fine.'

'Fine.'

'Could try get some jetskis.'

'I thought you said one day at a time.'

'Just thinking out loud.'

'Thinking, ya reckon? You reckon they'll let us just take a ski?'

'I don't know.'

Taj turns back to the shore. To the ocean and its endless horizon. Who the fuck cares what they do? These are gonna be the best days of his life.

Middle

Tonight's the night.
—Mick Fanning to Taj Burrow, Namotu Island, Fiji

Laying for a Day

Namotu, Fiji

TB: We had this ongoing joke, which came from Mick Fanning to start with, it was—we'd just kinda be talking about which night would be the night, you know, to celebrate. It ended up being quite a few. But every night Mick would just end up going, 'Tonight's the night!' [LAUGHS]. We ended up just saying that repeatedly, 'Tonight's the night', because we kept trying to pick one night but it ended up being several. It was just the most fucked-up perfect ingredients I could ever ask for. So we just acted accordingly. We got blind and we had the best time. We did all sorts of activities. We just lived it up on this island and had the best time.

JS: Is there anything that stood out in that gap between rounds?

TB: It's a bit of a blur. [LAUGHS] But we ended up just having so much fun but ... I don't know. I guess the one thing that really stood out to me the most, and I guess it's a fairly general thing, but it's ... the one thing I noticed the most was when I announced my retirement, amongst all my peers like that, when I announced my retirement I'd obviously let my guard down competitively and I just wanted to appreciate everyone as my friend. Because over the years, you know, I haven't been best mates with people like Mick Fanning, and guys that I'm just really competitive with, we're all mates but we've all just wanted to fucking rip each other's throats out when we get in the water. It's a weird one. But I feel as soon as I announced my retirement it was as if our guards had been dropped and we were just able to enjoy a friendship. And it was so noticeable to me. It was the most noticeable thing to me in my whole retirement how I just became friends with everyone way better. In the past, I guess I'm pretty cagey too, but I always have fun on tour, and everyone is still my mate, but I'm still there to beat them. And vice versa. We're all there to beat each other. So it's a weird friendship. I guess every competitor on earth would have the same thing but it was just the one thing I really noticed when we all just opened up and all became just actually friends. Where in the past it's almost like fake friends [LAUGHS].

JS: Was there anyone in particular that you felt you clicked with the best?

TB: Well, Mick, Mick was the example, for sure. I mean Joel [Parkinson] because we've spent more time together and we both ride for Billabong and so I've always been quite close with Joel. But it was even with Joel as well, since I retired we'd just start headlocking each other and laughing and there's no mind games being played, there's no bullshit, you know, you're mates and you're having a good time and celebrating all the years we've had, which is so many. But it was everyone across the board, but Mick and Joel were my main rivals across my career so those two I noticed the most.

The night's well lit. Burgeoning heat radiating from the tall standing lamps spewing smoke from their heads, the orange hue of burning leaves; kerosene-free, the black smoke lingers above them deterring mosquitos. And just like smoke, the look in Taj's eyes wavers with anticipation, he's been jumped plenty of times tonight and he's sick of smashing cocktails from used coconuts.

Sitting with his toes buried in the thick-grain sand, Taj admires the night. Caressed by the lick of crackling embers, a dry pile of driftwood is being poked with barbeque tongs, its resurrection slow yet no less amusing than Arabella's gibberish. It's a dream island this, fearless in its boasting.

Taj throws back his head and smashes the remnants of the frothy in his hand in salute. The stubby is short and fat, the label askew—folded with condensation—and now empty. Leaning in the green garden chair, careful not to lose his entire weight over the arm, Taj presses the base of the bottle into the sand. With pressure and gentle rotation, left, right, he forms the perfect triangle of discarded bottles. Find me a coconut and I'll take us all bowling.

'You want another beer, mate?' Joel's on his feet despite his knee brace, scratching at his chest with that trademark grin below an elongated nose. He stands with the fire pit to his back at the very moment the boys get it going. Fiery wings burst from Joel's shoulders and somehow that boyish smile turns devilish. Heat strikes Taj full-on in the face and of his mates he's the only one who immediately whirls out of his seat to seek safety.

'Fuck me,' Kai says, waving smoke from his eyes.

Someone caws over his protests.

Galahs. The lot of them.

'Nah, I'm right, hey,' Taj says, facing Joel. 'Getting bloated. These things are heavy.' That's when that devilish smile widens, and Taj feels his own face splitting. 'Fuck, alright.' He lets the laugh tear through him as Joel trundles over to the bar.

'Tonight's the night!' Mick cries, slapping Taj's shoulders as he treads in Joel's wake.

'Tonight's the night.' A chorus echoes.

Sponnas makes a gurgling sound from across the beach, he has that skull-shaped beer bong in his nimble fingers again and is spitting brown shit from his mouth as a chorus erupts around him. Short as he is, the tube protruding from the skull is nearly as long as he is.

What day is it? Taj finds himself thinking, which is always dangerous. When's that swell s'posed to hit? Fuck, but I better keep better track of this shit. He finds his thoughts drifting toward the other island. What were they doing over there? The Tavarua crew? The Americans and the rest of them? John John and Kelly and Tavarua. Is their bonfire as big as this? Are their nights *the* nights? What would Kelly be thinking right about now? Probably about that wave pool he's got cooking. And then that thought only makes Taj sweat. I'm retiring. I'm retiring. Where's my wave pool? Now that Kelly's there, he can't get rid of him. That's the thing about legends, they have that uncanny ability to linger well after their time is due to fuck off. The rivalries Taj and Kelly have had over the years have been tumultuous, back and forth, at each other's throats. By the gods nestled beneath the waves of this damn gorgeous ocean, if it weren't for Kelly, Taj could've been world champ a couple times over. Ah, but then Andy would have stepped up to the plate, more like. That's the thing about the tour: intimidation is part of the routine, right alongside ducking cameras and avoiding officials when you've had too many brews. And when the hooters are dormant and you're stuck at the same beach with your competitors, cameras packed down, smiles slip right off their faces just as easy as the jersey. He stops his thoughts dead as words reach his lips; monologue-ing on a session of beers is one of the more interesting feats of life, one he'd rather not partake in right now. Everyone's a philosopher on the grog. Or a dickhead.

'Here ya go, mate.'

Taj is handed a skull—without a cranium—over-brimming with a murky kinda clouded liquid. Joel's other hand holds a similar concoction, different skull. Joel has a knowing look in his eye. Taj presses his frothing skull to his lips.

'See ya at the bottom, ya old bastard,' Joel says.

It's vile, this fucking swampy drink, and boy, could it fuck a grown man stupid. A couple of these and you'd be able to fuel a tinny with nothing but your piss, and it'd still be better to the kilometre than E10.

Staring at the last of the skull's gunk and contemplating pouring it into the midst of his bottle-pins, the floaties and bubbled liquid, Taj shakes his head and yet still prefers it to the local brew, the kava. The root the locals grow on islands like these. Nurture the things for months and months then pull them from the ground, smash the chunks into a fine powder and throw it back with a handful of water. Kava's like the reverse to this drink. It starts up here and throws you on your arse faster than going over the falls would, it gives you the buzz, sure, but those Fijians here love the shit. Really love it. All over the island, without fail, you'll hear the holy cupping of their hands—*puh puh puh: Mathe!* The mild local narcotic is a traditional ceremonious partaking. It's also a favourite relaxant.

Taj laughs as he pulls the skull from his mouth, lips parted as the final wash of cloudy cocktail gushes the back of his throat. The skull in his palm is of similar size to the coconut cups the Fijians make you drink kava from, and although whatever this is tastes questionably better than dirt, he recognises, as his lips draw back into a snarl, that he feels the same rush to the head.

'What the fuck was that?'

'No idea,' Joel laughs, as he drops his own skull cup and wrestles Taj into a headlock, laughing like a lunatic.

'Tonight's the night,' someone shouts.

'Tonight's the night,' someone echoes.

TB: Oh! I had a mohawk at the time too. And one of the nights we had there, someone went, 'Fuck, you've got to cut so-and-so's hair.' And then people would put their hand up and be like, 'Yeah, shave my head too,' and I ended up giving about thirty mohawks. And everyone was just so ... like, we were drunk, and we were all having the best time of our lives, and I ended up doing all these mohawks. I ended up going through three or four sets of clippers. Everyone ended up having one.

Looking down at the third broken pair of clippers, hair tickling the top of his feet making him look as though he's on a cheap set of a Hobbit film, he can't contain the laughter any longer. How many fucking haircuts has he just given? This has to be some sort of record. The most amount of mohawked delinquents on one island! And at the helm, Taj Burrow steering them all to heck. Shit, he's done so many he can't even remember who'd been the first volunteer—the first sacrifice. Who'd even shouted the suggestion? There isn't a damn bloke on this island without a mohawk, and if they don't have one yet, they're lining up for one. Fuck, they better be. I've got another set of clippers coming down! Thinking about it, where are all these sets of clippers coming from?

With his sturdy hands, Taj grabs the dead clipper's head, choked with thick salty hair, and tears it free. Dropping it onto a pile of debris, shit like dreadlocks, empty bottles, plastic wrappers and the like, he opens his palm as the fourth set arrives.

'You're up, Joel,' Sponnas is saying, guiding the 2012 world champ to the wooden bench on the sand. Taj stands over the back of him, haunting with a smile, the electric buzzer vibrating like a set of bees. But Joel, wearing that trademark grin, drops onto the bench.

'What are you talking about, mate? You started this all with that fucking skull drink.'

'Didn't think I'd be getting my hair cut,' Joel says.

'It'll grow back. C'mon, you can't be the only one!'

'I'll do it for you, just don't fuck it up.'

Taj throws his hand onto Joel's forehead and rips his head back, as if he were a sacrificial lamb … the smiling sacrifice.

'Cut him,' everyone's chanting.

Joel's hair is short already, doesn't have a mop, but unlike the others, his hair is thick, consistent all the way through from forehead to the nape of his neck. Typical dad cut, bloke cut. No wonder the clippers are choking up. This is what Taj has been missing. The camaraderie of a few days in paradise, the fucking goddamn backstabbing in ceasefire and everyone's hair is down.

And gone. Mingling in foreign sands, on a foreign shore, they're brothers.

Taj cuts a clean path over Joel's scalp. This is a channel, smooth as a shaper's stroke.

And through the channel, thick with black hair either side like the parted sea, run Joel's fingers—sliding over the white skin there.

'C'mon, get the rest of it,' he says.

So Taj hacks into him some more.

The sun's rising and a few of the Brazilian competitors are already up and about juggling a soccer ball on their knees, each shout sending a shockwave to Taj's skull. Each cry, or dive in the sand, a bitter slap, a mourning for slumber. The new sun on his face is unkind. The room fan jiggles, creaking with each slow turn and the sweat pooling in Taj's folds speaks volumes.

He's wearing nothing but a sheet and a cloud of regret raining distorted memories.

A slow hand, a bottle of water and prawn crackers. He rinses them around like a garbage disposal between his gums, but what the hell did he eat last night for his insides to be roiling like this? He doubts he even ate. He knows the churning in his guts has nothing to do with whether he did or didn't.

Phone in hand, he stares at a photo of Rebecca, of Arabella. Of his family.

And acknowledges the rock concert pounding against his ribs. He has an appointment with Ronnie.

Nostalgia

Namotu, Fiji

Fiji is considered by most of the boys as the best event on tour, I think. And it's my favourite event so it was perfectly fitting to call it my last.
—*Taj Burrow, post–Fiji Pro 2016 WSL interview*[3]

Funny how he'd never imaged that he'd be departing the WSL tent with his every career memory so presented as to leave him speechless, dethroning him to the harsh reality of his uncertain future. The man with the fresh mohawk, and the sun-kissed skin, a one-year-old daughter and those others he loves waiting for him back home, understands the meaning of what has just taken place. It was a tribute, as if he were already gone. A reel of his life as if it needed flashing before his eyes. If he is to stumble across the footage again, as he surely will in the future, how will he watch this recap of his life and not feel so … sad?

Ronnie Blakey takes him back to the very start. Cameras stare like wide-eyed teens, lights pour a brilliant glow over his sweating chest and Ronnie smiles a knowing, coordinated smile. 'Ready?'

The interview begins.

Born on the coastal stretch of Busselton nearly four decades ago, Taj is lost in the grip of memories. Busselton, his birthplace, and the raw coastal land made awesome by its abundance of green and clean air. Busselton is where some say it all began for Taj but it was not the beginning of his legacy, per se. It was the subsequent town, Yallingup—a move that was the result of his parents Nancy and Vance's love for open, uncrowded waves. In 1974 they'd moved from San Diego, California, to escape the crowds and live the wayfarer sorta dreamscape. They began their journey in Perth. His mother worked as a waitress while his father, a young muso with a tendency for collaborations, gigged his way across the city and its suburbs. But in the end Perth was too reminiscent of the city life they left behind. Vance and Nancy migrated south to where the waves were bigger, the line-ups less populated and the land was open.

Seventy-eight was the year it began for Taj, not the year he took to the water, that wouldn't take place until he was seven, but it was the year life began. Apprenticed in his old man's arts—music and the way of the water—Taj remembers his first wave.

In Yallingup, in the place Taj still calls home, was a break where the reef—when the conditions were right, with the tide high and the swell big—makes the white water trickle, roll slow toward shore. He remembers standing up above the reef, hands spread out in a poo-man stance, remembers the look on his mum's face as she fist-pumped the air from the beach with a scream breaking from her lungs. The shouts from his old man egging him on from behind, still waist-deep in the waves where he'd pushed him off. Little did he know he had just launched his son into his destiny. From that instant, that moment of adrenaline from the first second he soared across the water's top to the very second he fell from the board's grip, Taj was hooked. And like with every surfer, the first wave was too quick. Taj needed to feel that rush again, and again. And again. One more wave is never enough.

Two years later Taj was competing in his first local boardriders contest. At nine years old he was itching to compete, but being thrown in the under-eighteen division was far from ideal. That didn't stop him from destroying the competition and winning his first-ever contest, taking down guys almost twice his age. Those days were the beginnings of his career.

It wasn't long until Colin from H2O Surfboards was shaping for him, and not long after that Rip Curl was throwing him wetties and Quiksilver was sending him wads of clothes. He thought he'd made it.

Taj smiles, trekking back to his bungalow, remembering how he'd go to school with the sticker packs his sponsors would send him. He became that little bit more popular. Until the sticker packs started to go missing. I know the chick who took 'em, too, he thinks, laughing.

Of course Maurice Cole came up, didn't he? In Ronnie's interview. Not directly, but it had to be answered with his mention. Turning down the tour, what was I thinking? Risky move you wouldn't contemplate nowadays. Maurice had been Taj's shaper and manager at the time when the ASP made their original offer. Taj was young then, sixteen, seventeen, and was out of his league when it came to the big world beyond Yallingup. On a not quite selfless decision, Maurice had encouraged Taj—when he was first approached by the world tour—to turn the offer down.

And boy, was there a repercussion. Good luck trying to qualify again, they said.

'Ah well, good riddance to him,' Taj murmurs, thinking back to his then-manager.

Taj had tried to keep the conflict between himself and Maurice contained, although that became harder and harder to do. The only positive thing he can take from it, he supposes, is the fact that he graduated high school. And not just make it to grade ten then pull the pin to get a trade, but make it all the way to grade twelve and walk out of there with a high school certificate and a stoked parent on either side of him.

The determination he had was unparalleled, as would become evident.

It was the year his world would change: 1998 he snagged the position in the Championship Tour. He toured the world. He surfed his brains out and was the youngest bloke out there every time. He was surfing in bouts against the likes of Mark Occhilupo,

Andy Irons, Tom Whitaker. Too many to name, more than enough to let the intimidation game scare the shit out of him. However, true to his character, Taj prevailed and was crowned the CT's Rookie of the Year.

Well, as it turns out, Taj thinks, looking over the beach toward the distant reef known as Cloudbreak, once a rookie always a rookie, because he has no idea what to expect next.

End

Generations upon generations of kids have been inspired by Taj Burrow. He's going to be greatly missed.
—*Martin Potter, post–Fiji Pro 2016 WSL interview*[4]

The Morning

Namotu, Fiji

In the grey gloom of dawn, Taj grinds his teeth as he kneads cream against the sting of his twitching muscles. The journey from bed to bathroom has never been further. Limping as his legs wake. Arms either side of the basin. The hangover's worse. His gut wrenches, twists and, for lack of a better word, screams. Taj's heart beats to the thrum of a headache. He's going to vomit but instead dry heaves. The morning air is warm. Sweat pools in the crevices of his evolving dad-body, perspiration bubbles burst beneath his puffy eyes. Traversing channels across tight leather-tanned skin, the sweat leaves a mark on his cheek, grinding across salty pores. Chafe rubs as he crouches, between his legs, under his arms, even his testicles. He exhales, blowing out his cheeks like a tired balloon and stares at his own eyes dead in the fogged mirror. The hangover's worse, and alcohol has nothing to do with it. No. The culprit is nerves and the assault has only just begun.

Taj drops onto the bathtub's edge, running a hand through his hair, and resumes rubbing cool cream into the back of his legs. 'Shit,' he says. John John Florence. His heart is in his throat. Of all the possibilities, of the outcomes to unfold, the man he's to face in the third round is the current world number three. Undoubtedly the deserved number one.

John John Florence is a young Hawaiian, blond and shaggy of head with an oversized jaw, he dominates with fear. His hairless chin, dark blue eyes above a straight-nosed pale face that looks too calculating, calm no matter who stands before him. Reminiscent of a young Kelly with a slightly introverted quirk to his nature.

Florence's surfing prowess is an acrobatic combination of

precise aerials and smooth, rail-gripping drives. His barrel game is strong. Nothing Taj can't combat if it comes to tube rides; if it comes down to anything at all, it'll be the waves themselves; Mother Nature and the pulses she throws.

The swell has begun to swoop in, and the winds are blowing steady, the tides are collecting and the ocean calls.

No.

Cloudbreak beckons.

Prepared or not, Taj straightens and looks himself dead-eye in the mirror and shouts, 'Prepared or not!' Taj feels the veins pulse in his neck as his voice deepens. 'Prepared or not.' Taj grips either side of the basin. Prepared for a showdown like he's never known, today is the day the world of surfing will stop, hold its breath and pray; not for Taj, but for the clock—for the clock to slow its count—for the reign of Fiji that is about to be throttled and Taj ready to overthrow.

John John won't see me coming.

The history books saved a page for this day. For this day will go down as heat of the year. Taj doesn't know it yet, but it's the final heat he will ever surf.

Round Three

Cloudbreak, Fiji

I was a little bit uneasy because I was just a little bit nervous on how it's all gonna unfold, I didn't even think about performing well, I kinda just forgot to surf. It probably hasn't really sunk in but then again I really am looking forward to it. I don't feel competitive anymore, I much prefer the part where I'm having a beer with all the boys and just kinda relaxing. All the boys have shown so much support and they all high-five me and give me the best vibe, it's just such a good feeling. And just all my friends and family—and fans— it's so cool to see how many people will support surfing, and me as well. You forget sometimes when you're in it and then you feel all this love coming from everyone and it's incredible. So I'm … really happy.
—Taj Burrow, post–Fiji Pro 2016 WSL interview[5]

It all comes down to this. No-one is left breathing, no-one dares prod the animal. The rocking is nauseating, stiff bones like rigor mortis, the afterblow of each turn is a battle, not an arrow fires astray. The war has begun.

Strike for strike, the surfing of round three is a massacre. No-one treads into this pool, a bloodbath, and Taj is soaked. Dripping from his fangs, nails dirty and eyes as wide as a frenzied dingo, salt stings the nostrils and he likes the taste of its burn. John John is no better, rabid with his slashes, relentless sprayage and brutal hacks as he traces his fins across the waves of Cloudbreak. The screaming mouths of the waves, the beasts cannot contain either of them, cannot—they won't let it be so!—and so they bury in its throat so deep the only out is to be spat with its roar.

The ocean's surface is scattered with the white remains of

giants, and so the waves scream as they're torn apart and return only to be bigger than before, and the judges can't keep up, and their pages are thrown with the speed of battle.

Taj and John eye each other from across the break, dripping with each other's lifeblood, their livelihoods on the line, the world is forgotten, all that matters is the fight, and it's Taj's turn to thrust. Cloudbreak screams. Welcomes him for a final roll of the dice.

The coast looks further away. With rolling white walls blocking the thrashed tree-lined utopia and adjacent reefs and sandbars overgrown with mangroves, the islands beyond may as well be home, a place of sanctuary and calm. The sea holds none of that today. A roll of foam the colour of polished bone sails into the distant gutters of the ocean and dies with a weak pulse. From the back of the break, Taj can see beyond the sponsor tower where inlays of sand moor him, and it reminds him of his own depth.

He's jealous his ankles are not buried on that shore, his family clinging to his arms, so free, he imagines the waters of Yallingup— and the waters he bleeds for. Yet this place, where lively islands await, would make for a fine holiday. Taj never thought he'd be dreaming of escape as he does now. An escape where surfing is furthest thing from his mind.

From the tower, Taj and John John are tiny pinpricks in the sea, amidst the gentle, rocking tide, paddling frantically as they fill the atmosphere with a familiar, infectious intensity; they achieve this with only their presence.

This does not seem right, a war as graceful as this. It shouldn't look like this. From the tower, it feels as if the instruments of a dream are role-playing, and smiles are currency.

A good day to witness a fight from a tower. A good day to face down the end.

'Now that's maximising time behind the curtain, Joe.' Potter says.

His co-commentator Joe Turpel nods his approval. 'John John straight out of the gates.'[6]

Everyone has made it from Namotu. The kitchenhands wear golden jerseys, the maids, the concierge, the barhands and the guides, they bounce on boats with 99s enough to total the phone book. Jerseys tight on their frames, they cheer and they aren't alone.

The electricity is unparalleled, and it spurs Taj to surf as if the volts are delivered direct into his bones. Even Mick, who has just surfed, has paddled back to the host of Aussies, Fijians and supporters from around the world, just to add his voice to the chorus.

John John, who has been training with Bede since the Quik on the Gold Coast, has just been spat from a wave, he goes down in the end bumps, but judges tend to overlook that.

He'll be scored with enough weight to force a lead change (8.17). Cloudbreak has shown up, it arrived with peaks double overhead, hollow barrels and fast lines.

It's time for Taj to answer back. He shoots through the back section of a blue line stretched out like an accordion to pull into a deep barrel. Seconds after John John has taken a dive off his board, Taj is caved. Two seconds wander by before he's thrown forward, fluidly slicing through the water like a knife through butter, he attacks with a trademark bottom-turn–top-turn combo, righting the manoeuvre with a backhand carve up the top of the lip—but Taj wants more; eyeing that lip line he carves it back to the source and reels as water graces him on all sides, like a dancer floating through silks; following through, coasting his way to the channel, he dives for the waiting ski (8.0).

'Well if there was any question whether Taj was going to take this heat seriously, then there's your answer,' says Potter. 'I think we'll see the lead change.'[7]

Unlike round one, he hasn't missed an opportunity, but John John won't be so forgiving—John John is considered the best in the game, and it sure as shit feels that way to Taj. He knew coming into this round he'd have to surf like he hadn't surfed in years. He wasn't quite sure he was up for it. All that scepticism is dead and gone now. And so, while Taj rides a jetski, he ignores his own rationale and John John upholds his reputation.

There are only waves. Fragments of other-worldly notions come and knock that thought from the pedestal every so often, like when Taj took off on his first wave of the heat. What a riot. So caught up in the goal he forgot to journey—he blames the nerves. Eighteen years on tour, thirty years surfing, he forgot how to surf. Not the 'oh, I'm gonna go out there and just go with the flow' forgot how to surf, he literally just forgot to think, he blanked.

Blankd up and went straight on a six-foot barrelling wall of pearlescent water. Talk about kook of the day, not the ideal opening to a round.

Time and again he finds he's almost paralysed by the idea of fear, overcome by anxiety, as the clock unwinds and he watches his career slip through his fingers as easily as running water. Mindful of the fact he has a job to do, he senses this about himself and is pleased. He laughs. Taj is having a ball! What is there to stress about? It takes the best kid in the world to push him to his limits, to open him up again and prove he isn't just a wash-up but worthy of a place on tour. The WSL will miss him … but not as much as Arabella will if he stays.

He's had too much to feel right now, and it seems not even surfing Cloudbreak will shake distractions free.

So, the battle must go on. The epic continues. John John's move. The scores draw closer.

Taj feels alive.

'And we'll see another lead change,' Potter says, to the delight of Joe in the booth beside him.[8]

John John's unique hardly-any-arm-movement kind of style commands his last wave as he drags, engages, his body with the water, shifting momentum, owning barrels. You'd be hard-pressed to find anyone who can get as deep in a tube. Taj accepts the fact and throws out what arsenal he has left as the cheers dancing on the wind spur him onto his next wave.

He endures a bouncy take-off by gripping rail and pulling hard left.

The barrel closes over his head and begins to tighten, he maximises the time he's got, not so hollow but he's squeezing in before launching with the spit in a dirty exit, a bounce breaking through the wall; the line stays open as he sets up. He wriggles in a carve to align a massive vertical backhand, hammering on the lip, jamming it right there, getting as vertical as it gets.

Not done yet.

With speed still on his side, Taj drives rail across the face of the wave, the crystalline blue cut with accurate, calculated manouevres.

The backside-rail work as he finds and slices the section is guided by the whoops of the wellwishers. Feeding off the love, the energy, he's not giving in without a fight.

The judges nod to each other (9.20).

Potter marvels as Taj turns off the shoulder, employing keen strokes, for the ski. 'Another lead change, Joe, guaranteed.'[8]

John John answers back alright, the judges still tallying the numbers and Taj isn't waiting around on results, he's surfing, the scores are wind, the opinions void, he's surfing, surfing and that's just what he does. John John's still attacking his wave when Taj takes off on a double overhead screamer and pulls in for a quick tube ride. He proves his worth, his position on tour, and jams a carve across the monster before ripping a huge backside tail drift to end the line; he gets out of there, jumps on the ski.

Two minutes pass and there's nothing wrong with using priority. He goes for wave of the day, it's colossal, more than double overhead, closer to ten foot than anything else, and it's clean and inviting.

Taj paces himself from the take-off, he knows what's coming.

The wave is forming and opening its maw. He slips into the tube as it hollows out, a birth of turgid water, spitting and thrashing as it pits itself into a heavy, giant barrel. The entire channel is freaking out. Somewhere John John is surfing ahead but Taj knows he's just cleared something special.

Shooting from the barrel, close to seven seconds from when he'd entered, he stands tall, faces the cameras and throws his hands out to the side: *How about that!*

But the wave is not done, he takes a look at the lip as it's forming and goes to give it a crack; that's when the rail digs, his body language too nonchalant, and he falls head over feet.

John John's wave is scored. He's taken the lead. Taj needs a 9.56.

'Taj needed a 9.56, he got a 9.40 so that little mishap at the end of that wave could be the difference that it comes down to.' Potter removes the headset.[10]

And so it's ended.

Taj crosses the tight gap and looks John John Florence in the eyes.

He's the first person Taj embraces as the hooter sounds, and he's a retired man.

A Man Above the Reef

*That was one of the best heats of my life. I could not have picked a
better way to finish my last event ever. The waves were exactly how
I'd want them and John John is exactly who I'd want to surf against
in those types of waves; someone who will push me to do my best.*
—*Taj Burrow, post–Fiji Pro 2016 WSL interview*[11]

As a man above the reef, between uncertainties, it gushes in on
him. Attacked by his own memories, the sensation of falling is
immediate and dangerous, and he labours in the tube of time,
back to the start of the end.

It doesn't feel right to break down here, to look over the tops
of people with hands on their heads, aghast faces, and let emotion
overcome you. The scores are coming in and it's way too close to
call. All Taj can find to centre himself is the slow, unenthusiastic
paddle back across the reef to the boats, anchored above the quiet
reef.

The scores are coming, and it's fucking close. John John had led
the bout from the start, though a part of Taj knows he's come a lot
closer than John John would have liked. Even as the curtains close
on an eighteen-year-long performance, and the scores are tallied,
marked and called, Taj fails to find fault.

The beer that's handed to him never tasted so good. He doesn't
even remember who gave it to him. And so he floats. Waiting.

The body slumps, with eighteen years of pressure sliding off into
nothingness, the spirit sings, free, peaceful as it drifts away into
the beyond in an effortless gift of goodbye. This, Taj knows, is

a feeling a long time coming, and not too dissimilar to peace. There were other times when he knew his soul had sung. But this had been building up inside his chest too long, filling him from the very moment he first stood up on a board, growing and swelling with every heat, every performance, too long it has grown, weighing on him like a burden, and now it has lifted on the wind, and he is free.

The applause is deafening, the slap of the water thick, as the volume of hands multiplies against the surface waves lapping against the boats; they bob, surfers and rafts alike. The sound is familiar, though Taj has never heard a chorus like this, it makes him think of the people who got him to this moment, of the people over the years, remembered and forgotten.

It will be remembered. He sits in the middle of a circle, surrounded by strangers, peers, colleagues, surfers, boaters and the sea, in the moment he is officially sent off. He feels the need to hold onto the tears. Not yet, not while the cameras are here, not while he wears the jersey, not while Arabella and Bec wait for him at home. Yet his face is wet, and if the odd tear falls, who's to know? And if he is to shed a tear, only minutes after his final round, still in the water he's just given his life for, they will be for himself alone. One drop to weep for who he has been; a second for who he has become.

Taj finds John close by. He nods in gratitude, thunders applause fit for a boulder. There's Kelly, a glint of a smile on his face that reads, *I'll give you this*. Even a few of the young'uns he hadn't had a real chance to get to know, slapping the sides of boats with sun-beaten arms. Their faces ecstatic.

It's all too much, he tells himself, he's ready to be a dad and nothing but a dad, and perhaps a brewer. Time is slowed and even this celebration begins to feel mechanical in its way, not disjointed but on the cusp of routine, a rehearsal for the public's eye; but he knows this isn't an absolute truth, he knows it for what it is, it's the second before the real media-circus shit begins, the second before the interviews and the piece to camera and the quotes and all the other shit he'll need to do before he can really let it all wash over him. But that's what this is, isn't it? His time to breathe.

They're giving him his time, still in the water, in the 99, giving him the moment, the minute of peace he's been stumbling toward for eighteen memorable years. To relive every one of those years would be like being thrown over the falls, like a man out of his depth, floundering, trying to find his way to his feet, knowing the tides will break him, suffocate him until he's hung out to dry.

Sometimes the tour felt like that, sometimes he'd felt like that on tour. But despite it all, the tour has given him something remarkable.

There's so much to be grateful for. He feels his shoulders shake as he breaks down.

Taj's smile never slips, though his hands shake as he rubs them over his face. The applause is relentless. The chorus sings on the wind. Where has Taj's humbled spirit flown to? A place where ambition goes to rest? How can he hope to hold himself together? Pitching forward, he splashes his face with the warm waters, and though it's a failed attempt to hide the smile through his hands he does it again. Again.

A rocking chair, a picture book. A small room, a balcony overlooking the shore. Birds in the nest, singing a new song. It's funny how for months he's been thinking of this very moment, and now that it's arrived, all he can think about is home. Not sparing a thought for the heat with John, not sparing a second glance at the tower or the cameras there; all that matters are the faces around him and the next few steps onto the sand.

Meanwhile the girls in his vision smile there, in the rocking chair, on the balcony by the shore. The birds change melodies and suddenly he wishes for his girls. When the thought subsides, and he realises he'll be home soon, he remembers his hands over his face and drops them to the water. The rocking chair by the balcony, the girls there will have him soon.

And then he lifts his head up and fixes an eye on Mick.

'Congrats, mate,' Mick says.

Not because he's in denial—he shakes his head because he can't believe it. They're coming from everywhere now.

'Nice one, legend.'

'Eighteen years too short, mate.'

'Congrats, ya grommet!'

All this from so many people. Of course, Sponnas is there, Gannon, Mick, Joel, Jack, Jules, Gabe, Wilko, Ace … all their faces meld into one. The boats creak and a couple knock together, as if everyone's forgotten how pumping Cloudbreak is. Taj reaches up to the closest boat and high-fives someone in a replica WSL 99 jersey, *Burrow* on the back, his grin ear to ear. These are the moment's he'll miss, but are no longer the moments he lives for; these are just moments above a reef for a man who loves to surf. And it's an honour to have been supported for so long. The love he's received, well, it chokes him.

Looking around, he rocks back on his Mayhem and shakes his head a final time with a smile. Laying it out, it's a fairytale: the sun's high, the ocean glorious and the reef full of coral you'll find nowhere else. The perfect ingredients to a perfect ending.

All of this, from the moment the siren sounded to the moment he climbs aboard a boat, lasts just a few seconds. But they're seconds he'll never forget. Taj Burrow says farewell. Surrounded by competitors. Surrounded by friends. Surrounded by the sea.

Ready to go home.

Hold-down
Sam Carmody

I lie in bed, lights off, and feel grim. Like an astronaut, preparing to be propelled into darkness.

I'd often felt like that as a kid back home in Western Australia, the night before a surf. I'd think of the sea, and the beaches out of town my brother and father and I would drive to in the early morning. How in that moment while I lay there under the covers, the ocean waiting for us would be black. Sharks would be stalking just beyond the surf. Bronze whalers, tiger sharks, all moved in with the night. Schools of baitfish, huddled on the sandbank. Schooling. Swimming. Feeding. Doing it all under darkness.

And I'd think of an attack. See my blood in the water.

That sensation has been a constant in my life. The approaching shadow. In the ocean, a white shark is always somewhere nearby, swimming towards me. I'm perpetually in the half-second before impact. All momentum and impossible weight, arriving from somewhere unseen.

I never do see the shark. It is a sort of phantom. But that sense of it there, arriving: that couldn't be more real.

I haven't surfed in months. I am now living in Darwin, lecturing at the university.

The chirp of geckos echoing through the house. The warm Timor Sea down the road still, quiet through the flywire. The air outside hot and windless. Scrubfowl rummaging, flicking soil in the garden.

It is two am. And there I am again, awake, alone, adrenalised.

Brenton asked me to close my eyes. I worked at looking serious and committed to the session, not wanting to reveal any suspicion or doubt for risk of offending him. Brenton had a nice face, handsome and earnest. Lopsided farmer-grin. And an athlete's body. Rounded biceps. Polo shirt tucked in at his narrow waist. His wasn't the look of an intellectual. More salt-of-the-earth captain of a regional footy side. Even his name had disappointed me when I first learned it.

I had been hoping for greying hair. The soft belly of a book-worm; someone who looked like they did little else than think and read and examine. Someone who truly looked like they could crack the troubling puzzle of why, at thirty-three, I had felt I was coming apart. But I dismissed my earlier judgment of Brenton best as I could. I knew it was important to surrender oneself to the whole ordeal, place faith in the hand of the process and the practitioner.

I was well practised at the psychologist's appointment. I first went to one on the advice of a PhD supervisor, ten years earlier, after she had seen something worrying in a particularly extended period of inertia. A year after confirmation and I hadn't written a word on my thesis. Instead of driving to the university and using the desk I shared with another candidate, I had instead for months headed to the northern beaches of Perth on my own. I would roll out of bed just before or after lunchtime, grab my board and drive to the empty midweek carparks. The sea breeze already in. The winter ocean too cold for swimmers. No flags or clubbies on the beach. The odd beachcomber or retiree might have wandered by along the shore, but otherwise it was just me, sitting on my surfboard out beyond the breakers. Pondering the likelihood of a passing great white shark. The water so clear that I could see the dirt in my toenails and the ripples of sand on the seabed. And I'd sit out there for hours, hidden in the roll of a winter swell.

'I want you to imagine an earlier time when you've felt like this. When you've felt anxious.'

I searched for something, a time that I'd had this same great pressure on my chest. Shoulders braced. I guessed Brenton was wanting something from childhood. Freud's first five years of life.

Disappointingly, and predictably, I pictured a schoolyard. The schoolyard of my childhood in Geraldton. St Lawrence's.

Clichéd, I thought. Even fraudulent. Primary school hadn't been an obvious nightmare. I was never bullied. I had friends. Kids I sat and ate lunch with. I played Kanga Cricket with a big mob of boys on the parched oval most days in the summer. Transporting to this place seemed like a waste of time, for both Brenton and me. But I had something to continue the charade with at the least. I calculated in my head the time left in the session.

'I want you take in the what's around you, everything you can see.' My mind seemed committed to this image of a quadrangle, plain and unspectacular as it was. I was glad I didn't have to tell Brenton where I'd transported to.

I sat against a brick wall, summer sky faded above me. Air warm. Across the courtyard children sat together on wooden benches. Some played foursquare.

After some time I opened my eyes. I realised then that I had been crying.

I often open my eyes underwater when I'm surfing, during a duck dive, or when I bail off my board and swim under and through a wave, and I do it during a hold-down, too.

It is the moment after a particularly bad wipeout, after the wild, teeth-rattling explosion of water, the cartwheeling, the roar in your ears. Once the rumbling has subsided, replaced by a muffled quiet. When you might have expected to begin to float upwards toward the surface, when the water instead draws you deeper.

The hold-down is a slow descending. An amorphous downward pull. The grip of water on ever surface of your body, so all-encompassing that you could be fooled for thinking you were suddenly heavier, that it was your destiny to sink to the seabed.

I have always been someone more inclined to watch the world than participate in it. Which seems like an odd quality for a person when you write it down.

After dinner parties, when someone reaches for a board game or set of cards I'll do my best to get myself out of it. I'll fill my glass, set the chair back from the table and just watch.

As a child I was the sort of kid who crept around, loitered, stalked the bedrooms of the house when other people weren't home, someone who nosied through drawers. Borrowed things. Moved them. Like a phantom. A ghost. The way my older brother tells it, I was more an off-putting sort of younger brother than an annoying one. It was the feeling of being haunted, he describes, of being constantly watched.

I grew up in Geraldton, the harbour town four and a bit hours drive north of Perth. And being this voyeuristic kid, one of the things I loved to watch the most was the sea. I didn't necessarily love to be in it, or on it, as my surfer brother did.

In fact I've been wary of the sea as far back as I can remember. I cried the first time my dad tried to teach me to surf when I was about six, carrying me out above the small waves on a foam surfboard. It is one of the strongest memories I have, that sudden recognition that the ocean was bigger than even my father had seemed to me then. I'd felt the shadowy power of it. I remember screaming to the sky that my father was trying to kill me.

Despite the fear I had of it I still could never get enough of the ocean. I read all about the *Batavia* shipwreck. I'd watch Ron and Valerie Taylor documentaries about a big reef on the other side of the country that you could see from space. I'd watch my brother's surfing movies. And I loved nothing more than just to look through the sliding doors of our place, out over the train tracks, and stare at the water, marvelling at everything it concealed. The bones of Dutch sailors. Sharks. The ocean's surface an opaque green, like a sheet pulled over things that we might otherwise prefer not to see.

When Dad and Liam would get up before light on winter mornings, I'd get up with them. Rugged up in trackies, sitting in the back seat with the dog, listening to my father and brother's quiet conversation as we weaved out of town in darkness, eventually taking the sandy tracks and beaches in search of waves. Headlights tunnelling through the dark. The four-wheel drive lurching and bouncing. Sometimes it felt as if we weren't going anywhere at all, just spinning on the spot, the rear wheels drifting down towards the water.

At some point Dad would roll down the window and there would be the sudden chill of the night and the sea air. Stewing seaweed. Dead fish. Out the window there would be light enough to just make out the lines of swell. The surf still two-dimensional in the low light. Dark walls of water and then the flash of white as they broke.

When we'd finally stop, and Dad would kill the ignition, there'd be the full volume of the sea. The hiss of the shoreline. The boom of waves on the outer sandbanks.

I wouldn't get out of the car with them as they went to change into their wetsuits, it would be so bloody cold. Instead I'd move to the front seats, and look through a misted windscreen, and watch them surf a remote break for a few hours as the sun came up. I'd imagine myself out there with them.

What I loved most of all of it was the car ride home, Dad complaining about the farts of Spike, our Jack Russell. The iced coffee from the roadhouse. The KitKat. It is a peculiar thing—the feeling in a car on its return from the sea. Like returning from a war front. The mood triumphant. Everything under full sunlight. Roos bounding about in the dunes. The world boisterous with sound, with colour, as if it has gained confidence out of darkness.

Brenton and I waded around in this childhood territory each week. I tried to throw him all the Freudian bones I could summon. So I told him about the chair bag incident.

It was year three, in Mrs Bradley's class. She had just given an instruction and the class had leapt into action. I stood up with them. Like everyone else, I had run my hands through my chair bag, searching in the large orange sack that hung from the plastic back of my chair. The chair bag I remember was heavy, with snapped pencils and dead, lidless textas. There were stray pieces of paper and the bottom was lined thick with the gravelly sand of old, crushed biscuits. But there was no assignment. Whatever I'd had to find, that she had just asked for, was not there. Whatever task I'd had to complete, I hadn't done it.

And now Mrs Bradley waited by the carpet. One by one, the children joined her. They formed a wriggling circle on the floor. I can't remember what they had with them. I imagine some sort of show-and-tell. An assortment of sea creatures, dead and dying. Sea urchins and the chalky carcasses of cuttlefish. Cowrie shells. All sandy and sun-bleached and decomposing in the Geraldton heat, smelling of old shoes.

The activity began without me as I stood terrified by my desk. I crouched behind my chair bag, almost in disbelief that no-one had noticed I was absent. It was a ridiculous thing to think. Mrs Bradley must have known that I was hiding up there. Or perhaps she really didn't know.

The story goes that I hid inside my chair bag, like an orange cocoon dangling inches from the ground. That's the way Dan tells it anyway. It's a version that defies plausibility but that doesn't stop him. He loves that story. And he's got a kind of authority on the matter, too. After all, he was there, sitting down at the feet of Mrs Bradley that day in year three.

Dan and I have been best mates for as long as I can think and I must have heard him tell the 'chair bag' tale near on a hundred times. Each performance of it is rolled out with the same fresh enthusiasm, as though he's summoning the original moment from a vacuum bag. And it's not just that story. They're seemingly endless, these stories of me and the odd things I did.

In the mornings, I stay in bed until I hear the last of my house-mates' footsteps on the wooden boards, and the last car roll out of the driveway.

On the way to work I use the drive-thru at McDonald's to order coffee because the conveyor-belt customer service—the alarms and timers and humans running at capacity—rules out conversation or extended eye contact.

At work, I sit in my office with the door closed to avoid talking to colleagues. There is a big pair of scissors in my drawer and I snip away at my beard while I watch surfing movies on YouTube because I can't bring myself to open the digital pile of first-year essays.

On the whiteboard in my office, in blue marker, there is a list under the title 'opportunities'. Fulbright. Postdocs. A writing residency. The application dates scribbled next to them, all long expired.

I had always been good at daydreaming. It was the thing I loved occupying myself with most, or the thing I escaped with. In the midst of any sort of malaise I could feel suddenly buoyant with the visions in my mind. Of postdoctorates and fellowships and residencies in North America and Europe. I would muse about one day having a family. A kid I could put an arm around.

I noticed I'd lost this skill to dream things up. At some point, my sense of future weeks or months had disappeared, like a road washed away.

After six pm, when the university is safely empty and only cleaners are in the corridors, I pack up my things. I buy a sixpack of beer on my way home from the university and take it straight to my room, hoping to again evade my housemates.

And I lie on my bed, simultaneously numb and afraid. Sure of nothing at all except the feeling that death—like a great white torpedoing out of deeper water—is closing in.

Most of Dan's anecdotes recall our seven years in primary school. I'm not sure why. I guess he holds a fondness for those early memories of Geraldton, like most do for their childhood: vague, intoxicated memories, not burdened by adult realism or precision. In this way, primary school is convenient territory for his stories, a kind of storyteller's island, sufficiently isolated by time. Our primary school, St Lawrence's, has become a place with a seven-foot-tall catholic nun with a boxer's forearms. And in another story there is an overwhelmed student teacher who, in a desperate moment, screams so hard at her class she begins to levitate. As fantastic and mythical as these stories have become, I don't dispute them. Truth is I don't remember much of those years. I wish I did, although Dan's stories have, over the years, made for a pleasing substitute. It's a surreal and blissful picture he creates, like a Roald Dahl story, and I find myself, the central character of much of it, delighting in the joyful refuge of those tales.

I booked an appointment with a psychiatrist. His name was Richard.

In the long, rudderless days in the office at the uni I'd read reams of online articles on attention deficit disorder. I was convinced that was my problem. Why I couldn't seem to settle my mind on anything. Assignments that needed marking. Or some picture of the future.

The psychiatry appointment was via Skype. Richard in his office in Geelong, me in Darwin. He seemed more the part than Brenton. Glasses. Bald. A cultivated English accent. And, of course, he asked me about my childhood.

My memories of childhood and Geraldton have an indistinct, dreamy quality. Nothing is clear. It's all impressions and approximations, smells and feelings, and it makes me wonder if I ever paid attention to anything. I remember the trees around my suburb, tall eucalypts and peppermint trees, brawling with an afternoon sea breeze. I remember the crunch of dead lawn underfoot. The warm, green ocean. But that's all. Not street names or the names of neighbours. When I go back to Geraldton now, I'm quickly lost. The town seems jumbled. Back to front. I recognise buildings but it's as though they've been moved, cut from the Geraldton of my memory and sutured into a different street on the other side of town. After ten minutes in the car I've lost all confidence and the driving slows to a kind of tourist's crawl. I was there for ten years but somehow it's like I've never been there before. The place feels the same. The summer heat in my nostrils. The sea breeze. All that useless information.

Dan found my sense of direction hilarious. He moved to Perth five years after I did, after high school, but quickly gained a better feel for the city. Perth is a tangle for me, a mess of fishing line I've never sorted out.

My family made the move from the country when I was midway through year eight. It is an odd thing, but I recall those first few weeks at the new school in Perth in remarkable detail, clearer than any of the four years that followed. The school grounds were new-looking. Ramps instead of stairs. Yellow grab rails. Cream brick and stainless steel and glass. The winter sky was pale and clear. I can remember the vice grip of the morning air, how it drifted silently down the corridors, how it stiffened my back, and the icy dampness in my nostrils. At recess and lunchtime I did careful laps of the lockers, watching the other children. They sat in animated clumps, talk and laughter washing like surf through the courtyard. From the lockers I could see the ocean, a strip of blue above the corrugated roofing of the quad. Some days I would just stand there with my lunch and watch it. The water dark and still, never moving, trapped and subdued by the low shimmering wall of Rottnest Island.

A yarn Dan often recites is one that might be titled 'The Olympian Beer Bottle Throw'. It occurs one lunchtime in year two on the large lower oval of the school. Dan describes a typical scene. Children scattered across the length of the ground, yellow flap-hats almost white in the late-morning sun. A mob of older boys locked in a grim-faced cricket game on a shiny concrete pitch while smaller bodies hurtle and zip around them. I am standing alone on the bottom corner of the grounds where on one side the school runs into bush, and on the other, far beyond the fence line, on Chapman Road, utilities and road trains noisily rip through the humid air. What happens next can only be one of two things: either a horrific assault on a small child or a malfunctioning of a young imagination. In any case, it is true that I ran to the teacher patrolling the oval to tell them I'd been struck on the forehead by a beer bottle flung from a passing car on Chapman Road. My father was in his office when he received the phone call from the deputy principal. Something extraordinary had occurred to his son. He did the calculations in his mind as he heard what I'd told the teacher on the oval. The bottle had travelled a terrific distance, a hundred metres or more, projected from the window of a vehicle travelling at least eighty kilometres an hour; a triumph of the human arm. The deputy principal, Mr Boyle, reassured him I had taken it well, reporting only a mild headache and not a mark left by the blow. My father asked if they found the beer bottle to which Mr Boyle replied, no; it could not be found as it had bounced from my head a further fifty metres over another fence into thick scrub. There were no witnesses, the deputy principal told him. Not long afterwards my mother arrived at the school office to take me home.

When Dan tells the Olympian beer bottle story I can't help but laugh along with everyone. He does it so well. He's got a gift and I envy him for it. A real storyteller, in the tangible, stage-ready way a lot of writers I know aren't. Dan's not a tall guy and does not have the biggest voice but when he begins a story attention quickly gathers. People move towards him, drawn in like a tide. It's kind of miraculous to watch. And it's not just his exuberance, that beaming high-rev charm. Dan's stories jolt life into everything. A forgotten time thrives again. And weary, confused memories become almost beautiful. When Dan sets off, the world augments into something magnificent, and something I can make sense of. On my own it is never so clear. I wonder what was going through the mind of that boy on the oval, standing alone at the school boundary, watching the highway. Imagining wild and silly things. More and more I worry about him.

But I'm also grateful for Dan. The history he has constructed for the both of us. I don't know what I'd have without him.

My mind has always been elsewhere. Or maybe it has never been anywhere. All I know is that for much of my school and working life I've watched the teacher during a class, or a colleague or boss, seen their lips moving, and not heard a word. Thirty minutes can go by before I realise that I've been elsewhere. I hate the feeling. It's much like missing a bus, and rushing all around is the traffic of words and ideas that I should understand but don't. I spend the rest of a lesson feeling heavy and on edge, eyes down at the desk, hoping no-one asks me anything. I remember my five years of high school mostly for this feeling, a kind of dizzy, bewildered terror. And it wasn't just the newness of it all, the clutter of unfamiliar faces, or the city. It was as if my thoughts were caught up in a hot summer wind and I couldn't tie them down.

I learned to surf later that first year. I was never really the surfing type but one day I heard myself declare in front of a group of students that the surf 'went off in Gero'. This statement drew attention from the angry-eyed, scruffy-haired kids towards the back of the classroom, and although I'd never been interested in standing up on a surfboard it was clear I'd committed myself to learning how.

The ocean spooked me, the unpredictability of it. Entering the water was a contract I didn't trust. Waves broke deals. They were shifty and unreliable. I particularly didn't like the paddle out, running the gauntlet of the sandbank. My new friends would charge off like infantry, leaving me standing alone in the shallows of Trigg Beach, the board heavy under my arm. I watched the sea hard, stiff-backed and alert, assessing odds, waiting for the waves to quieten before I set off. And then when I thought I had got through it and paddled far enough out to sea, far enough to reach the calm beyond the breakers, sure enough the horizon would bloat and darken with a swell bigger than I had ever seen and I would wait in the shadow of it like a roo before a road train. But I soon grew addicted to it. That out of the chaos and danger of shifting water, you could find something meaningful. Perfection, even. After whole days in the fog of the classroom, in the snarling tangle of your thoughts, sometimes the ocean was the only thing that made any sense.

'Sam, you fit the criteria for inattentive-type ADHD, which a psychiatrist can treat with medication,' Richard said. 'But I'm really less concerned about that. I think you have a major depressive disorder. I want you to go on medication.'

I booked a flight back to Western Australia for the wedding of my first real girlfriend. There was never a question of whether or not I was going, as expensive as flights out of Darwin were. As strange as it might have sounded to be so sure about something. But I was always going. Not just for the wedding, but the surf too, and the chance to see family.

But also, it was something to look forward to. An increasingly rare appointment with the future.

In the lead-up to going I found myself telling people. Watched their reactions. I told them how Sally called me when she got engaged. That her fiancé was somewhere in the room there, too.

How did I feel about it? The whole wedding thing? I mean, it must be weird?

Truth was I was proud of it. That ten years later I'd still be close to all of them in some way. It felt like it said something important that she'd want me there. It was also a proximity to some younger me, when the picture of who I was and where I was going was more solid.

I spent too much money on my outfit. A baby blue linen jacket. A bow-tie. Dangerously close to something from an old-school gameshow. I took a photo in the fitting room mirror, revisit it. Sometimes I saw off-beat cool, sophistication. A Bond throwback. Other times I was a shitty version of a crooner from the '60s. But the girl at the clothes shop in Darwin was sure about it. 'It's fun,' she said. 'You'll stand out.'

The night before the flight, after packing too late again, I struggled to sleep. Found myself reading about a shooting at a school in Kentucky. Some bloke is being pilloried, a school guard who hid behind the brick wall near the front office with his pistol while booms went off inside and windows blew out.

I'd sometimes imagine some American scene when walking around the university campus in Darwin. Which is a bit dumb because there are never any students around. But on the trips to the café at the foot of the library I'll conjure a kid wielding a gun. Me, charging out of his blind spot and knocking him down. Or leaping from a balcony one storey above and landing on his shoulders. I picture, too, the hospital bed interview. Some injury. A bullet through the shoulder, or a knife wound that just missed something vital. Critical at first, but not lasting. I envy the people in those interviews. Shirtless. And the right to be philosophical. I like to think that I'm in a fitness streak when it all goes down. Not over-muscled but lean.

It was weird being back in Perth. Mum and Dad had moved south to Yallingup. For the first time I didn't have a room or a car to borrow.

There was a small private ceremony for family beforehand. I booked a car from the hotel and arrived at the reception too early.

I walked down to where the sandy path to the beach began. Stood on the chalky timber fence in my new Oxfords. It was all whipping sand and wind and light.

The late-afternoon beach was deserted. There were a couple of bodysurfers in the shoreline. One surfer further out on her own, maybe a teenager, trying to make sense of the weak wind swell. She spun around on a knee-high wave and in an instant it was clear she was good, quick to her feet and somehow finding a fast line. But the wave was a dead end and dissolved to nothing, and she flopped off the back theatrically, like she'd been shot. She emerged lazily from the water and for a moment stood still on the sandbank, turned the small surfboard over in her hands, looked briefly to the beach, then paddled back out.

I envied her. The freedom of wasting time, bobbing over half-wave after half-wave, deciding which one to choose, like flicking through shitty TV channels.

I registered that she was out there alone, too, and a part of me envied that.

And I felt morbid, too, suddenly. The thousand afternoons I

spent like that in the summer wind swell, alone, when no-one in their right mind would bother. Wasting time.

I held and counted my breaths the way a therapist once showed me. One. One two. One two three. One two three four. I tried to not just be the guy posing as if he's looking out to sea but the guy actually looking out to sea. But my thoughts were all over the shop.

Sally's friends were the impressive sort. They were always going places. Over the years I'd followed their movements online. Richard who'd studied at Cambridge then founded an engineering NGO that got featured in the *New York Times*. Em, who ended up working in the prime minister's office.

I thought about what I'd tell them: my work teaching fiction writing in the far north of the country, my novel that was no longer on bookshop shelves.

Behind me, near the venue, there was a crowd gathering. The men were all in black. Wool coats. I half considered reefing the linen jacket off and leaving the fucking thing in the dunes.

They looked at me like I shouldn't be there. Or perhaps that was not fair, or entirely true. But they looked surprised I was there, which made me feel like maybe I really shouldn't be. And for the first time it was clear that all this had been a mistake.

At the reception, I sat at the table with the cousins and their partners. Nearly all of them married now. Except for Christabel, Sally's youngest cousin. Christabel and I talked shit like we always used to. She was quick to laugh and in fleeting moments it was almost like the old days. She was in early high school when I started dating Sally. Twenty-seven now.

I didn't talk to Sally. She got close on one of her rounds, hugging people. She gave me a smile from within a scrum. She looked beautiful.

Her new husband came up and shook my hand.

Later, I danced with Christabel. There were trays of shots brought out. It was the last thing I remembered.

Dan's anecdotes follow a familiar theme. There will be me, forgetting things. School lunches. Bathers for swimming lessons. Or drifting off, staring out windows or drawing in my exercise book, and often giving doomed recitals in front of the classroom of the lesson I'd not heard a word of. The stories have a sitcom's design: the familiar character in the familiar setting, doing expected things. Dan would tell them of the day the heavyweight nun lowered me into a classroom bin by my ankles.

In the running compilation of stories that Dan has kept about me, high school is the missing chapter.

I'm left with my own memories. That lack the comfort of a careful, amusing edit.

I think of my maths teacher, Mr Joyce. Squat. With hairy arms. Arms circled.

I'm up the back of class as if taking cover. Knowing what's coming, for once in no doubt. The assessments in the neat pile. Joyce plucking one from it like a weapon.

'Story of your life, Carmody,' he'd say after reading an underwhelming grade of mine out to the classroom.

And even though I was surrounded by my peers, I had felt already cut adrift. Like a fisher fallen off the back of a trawler. The other kids' sniggers washed about the room. I knew as well as they did that I was already floundering in their wake.

The morning after the wedding I woke in a bedroom in a house I'd never been in before. On the floor my once white shirt was a debacle—like I'd been bludgeoned across the spine with a beetroot—and there was beach sand in my shoes. I couldn't find my jacket. My phone and wallet and keys were in the inside pocket.

There were photographs on the wall next to the pillow. A self-portrait of Christabel on her back on a bright-green lawn with a dog in her arms. A pretty Australian shepherd kind of thing, coat mottled white and grey. In the photo it strains to lick her nose, eyes rolled back like a white shark.

There was of course no landline. Not that I'd know who to call, or would remember what their number was.

I walked around the house in my dress pants, circling like a madman. Had to sit down every dozen steps so I didn't spew.

In the living room I found the dog from the photograph. Shiny-eyed and expensive-looking. Purebred. The name on the collar said Flo. Flo was happy for the company as well and I hugged the dog on the couch. After a while Flo seemed suspicious that I was hanging around. Like I should be in the company of humans, or have somewhere else to be. Things to worry about.

Christabel came through the door. She'd been out with the family at an after-wedding breakfast. She didn't say anything about the previous night. She booked me a ride back to my accommodation.

When I reached Mum and Dad's in Yallingup, I planted myself on the couch. It was a feeling of such relief. But then something happened.

First, a sort of falling. Or was it the sensation of leaving the ground?

All I could say for sure was that the world was all of a sudden unreal.

Or maybe I was unreal.

All I could say for sure was that there was nothing I was sure of. Just that this feeling was no good. No good at all.

A cup of tea was placed in front of me. My parents' smiles were big and grateful. They were excited that I was there. But I was not really there.

I'd become aware of breathing. Hot and sour on exhalation. Thick, fumy. It was more like drowning than breathing.

There was the moisture at my wrists, on my palms. I moved my arms. I could move things, yes. Ordered my fists to close and they did.

'I feel a bit odd,' I heard myself say, in a tone attempting cheeriness.

Then my dad was sat next to me, fingers over my wrist. Like Mum, he was once a nurse.

'Your pulse is a bit boundy but it's fine,' Dad said. 'Have a lie-down.'

He helped me to my feet and guided me down the hall.

For the next hour I lay there in the spare room, trying to tether my mind to my body. And what mind was this? Observing details. Reporting on the strangeness of it all, like a terrified astronaut, flung into some miserable, unspeakable dimension. Because it wasn't my mind. I was somewhere else. Not far away, not yet, but unattached. Somewhere I might never return to. Untethered. Adrift.

And then it all turned, in a way; the axis of this feeling, it shifted again. Somehow worse. In a way that there was no defining. Just worse. Weirder.

Was this what dying was? This disintegration of a self?

That was the worst of it. How unexplainable it was. How could anyone help you if you couldn't describe what was going on? Like someone calling for help without coordinates of where they were. And that was terrifying, the thought of trying to find words.

It shifted again. It was such a hopeless situation I felt like crying and sensed my lower lip trembling. Then I'd stop, because the sensation of a lip trembling, separate from myself, felt so bloody weird I'd snap out of it. The horror was so great there was no crying.

I closed my eyes to attempt to sleep but there was no way. The mind that could sleep, that warmly enclosed my very being, was gone: in its place was an alert void. Alert—alive, yes—but not really. It felt like a machine in shutdown.

'There is a lot of performing going on.'

Brenton was describing the growing effort I felt with each interaction I had with others, be it strangers or friends: how it felt as though I had just walked onto a stage, and my performance could be judged.

Conversations about mental health in our family history, like many, I imagine, are coded with euphemisms. There's talk of 'melancholy' or 'neuroticism'. There's an alcoholic, long-dead relative. An eccentric grandmother who was prone to dark moods. But anxiety or depression are words I hadn't heard.

I reckon I've always lived with anxiety, with the engine of the mind running too hot. Thinking too much. Every conversation a performance that could be measured, adjudicated.

In the morning I woke, the feeling gone. Dad was there, before first light, already in the hall outside my door like a sentinel. He suggested a surf.

The salmon were running. There were sharks about. It's all that people had been talking about. Bronze whalers in the trench of the shoreline, often metres offshore, gliding through hollows and channels in the reef. Great white sharks further out, patrolling the surf line. A month before, an Argentinian surfer had been knocked off his board. Just last week a twelve-year-old was swiped by a tail. It's the limestone reefs, I think, that make it risky. Shelves and platforms that look almost black from above the water. Perfect cover for the dark back of a big shark.

My dad and I didn't surf on the reef but in the bay. Over sand. The spot is called Cyclops. On a big swell, all that energy is shepherded into the bay by headlands on each side. The waves climb out of deep water before lurching all leery onto shallow sand, and then it appears, briefly. Cyclops. Tunnelling down the sandbank. A violent, flaring orb. Like an angry eye.

But the swell was small. It was not really Cyclops at all; today the eye was closed. We could see surfers silhouetted up in the carpark but they didn't join us.

The morning sun came in low, flat spears over the ridge of eucalypts and tangled scrub. The easterly blew cold down onto the beach that was still in shadow. I was unfit. My arms quickly felt hollow from paddling, like there was nothing to them. I felt salt in the mosquito bites on my ankles. I was slow to my feet.

But it was the happiest I'd been in weeks. A wave came that was almost something like Cyclops. For a flash I was inside the eye, looking out. My head hit the ceiling of funnelling water and then I was cartwheeling. I came to a stop on the seabed, pushed down into a yogic pose on the sand. Eventually it let me up.

Dad and I bobbed about, just the two of us. Being alone in the surf anywhere these days is a rare enough thing. We felt imperious, which was problematic. My great-great-grandfather settled this coast in 1832. The small towns bear the first names of distant great-great-aunts.

In the carpark Dad and I talked about property. We drove around the houses at Yallingup Beach. Three million dollars. I'd go for the top one, when I hit some kind of jackpot. Though something smaller would be enough. A block somewhere tucked away from the coast.

'You could put a shipping container on it,' I said.

This kind of thing is Dad's favourite subject. Daydreaming. But I knew I was lying. I just couldn't see any of it.

During a hold-down the thing that unsettles me the most is the momentary blindness. How the combustion of water and air and misting sand creates a sort of visual static, a flickering screen, and one loses any sense of just where in the water column one is. A really bad wipeout—a snapped leg-rope, a busted eardrum—can leave you in doubt of which way is up at all. Surfers have paddled over to a stricken comrade to find them swimming underwater, clawing toward the bottom. Their instincts to survive suddenly the thing endangering them the most.

Depression, I think, is something like that. The utter disorientation. And the sudden untrustworthiness of your instincts. How your efforts to protect yourself might be the deadliest thing of all.

On the second day at my parents' house, I thought about unpacking my clothes, putting them away in the cupboards, but I left them in the bag and by the first afternoon they were across the floor. That murky feeling settled in. Where picking jeans up off the floor felt arduous. Cosmically difficult. Like I might disintegrate as I bent over. So I lay back on the bed with my phone. Flicking through dating profiles. The photos were mostly selfies, pixelated as if taken on cheap phones. And I wondered if they were selfies because no-one else had taken their picture, or they hadn't been invited into a photo for a long time, because they'd been alone too much. Posing alone in the dull light of a boxy apartment, low-ceilinged. Smiling and lonely.

I slept from midmorning to midafternoon. I could sense it was freaking out my mum, who waited in the living room for me. But even knowing it was hurting her, the worry, I couldn't pull myself from the bed.

When eventually I did, I phoned Richard. He wrote me a script and faxed it across the country. Later Mum and I drove into town. I felt embarrassed, as of course I knew I shouldn't feel. I knew there was no shame in depression or anxiety. But still, there was no denying that it was shame I felt, sitting there in the passenger seat next to Mum, in a strange throwback to the school drives and dentist appointments two decades earlier.

My parents have always been unenthusiastic about pharmaceuticals. Suspect on the idea of them, the same way people can be about a microwave. It's unnatural. But in one day Mum had turned on the idea of antidepressants. Which shamed me further. That the sight of her son lying on the bed in the spare room fearing he'd lost his mind might have been enough to change hers.

That afternoon I took Mum's car to Cyclops on my own. The wind was now onshore, but the eye was still there. Emerging out of the chaos of the sea. A loan bodyboarder tackled it. I envied him. His courage.

At the southern end of the beach a fisherman reeled in the top half of a salmon out of the shore break, ribbons of blood trailing behind it.

I've heard of surfers who don't come up from a hold-down. Pulled toward the bottom and held there, unable to get to the surface before another wave passes over them and they are pushed deeper.

I wonder how dark it might get, then. Sunlight gone, blocked by whitewater.

One morning in my apartment in Darwin I sit on the couch and I feel a heaviness I've never quite experienced before. It is the vertigo of a hold-down. The slow downward pull. But deeper, somehow, like I am no longer really in the world.

I remember feeling drawn to the garden shed at the side of the building. Such a drab, domestic scene. Quiet and hidden. Out of view of my neighbours or the street.

I text Brenton. Leave the house, as if trying to run from myself.

'He feels different, that boy,' Brenton says. 'He feels defective.'

He is talking of the child in the school quadrangle.

'That is a lonely, scary way to feel.'

Brenton asks me to close my eyes. He tells me to find the eight-year-old me sat against the brick wall and sit down beside him.

I do as he says. I lower myself down next to the boy in his grey school clothes. I see his freckly, scabby knees. I see the fear and shame in his face.

I put my arm around him.

A year later and I'm no longer on medication. And I'm no longer in Darwin. I accept a journalism gig on the southern coast of Western Australia, and move back nearer family, nearer a surf coast. My brother lives in the next town to the west, and on weekends we search for waves, four-wheel driving along empty bays and down narrow fishermen's tracks.

There will be another time to write about all this, I hope. Where some insights on it all are clearer. Maybe there will be a tidy conclusion. Because if I'm honest, I don't feel recovered, or sure about the future. More wounded by the recent past. Relieved of course, but frightened about how close I came.

But beyond uncertain metaphors, surfing has been the thing I've reached for. Right now, it is the thing my life revolves around. I ordered new boards off a shaper in Yallingup, and now have more boards, more wetsuits, more wax, than a 'weekend warrior' should justifiably have. But with surfing, things are simplified. Weeks lived around weather systems. The five-day forecast. One's vision is never cast too far forward.

Of course there are lots of moments when I'm the guy bobbing around out the back in the surf, looking out to sea, wanting to be the guy just looking out to sea. Not the one thinking of sharks, worrying about hold-downs. Or feeling somehow defective. That I've come up short.

Finding hope in the future remains work. It is a daily practice.

But I like opening my eyes under the water. Here, when a wave is breaking overhead, the ocean is a white-blue. Electric, almost. Those seconds underwater are when I feel most in the world. They're moments of genuine clarity and presence—the purest joy I know.

Notes and references

Following the Birds—Madelaine Dickie

1. Dave ran surfboard shaping workshops near Wollongong in NSW as part of his business Treehouse Landscapes and Handshapes. He helped me shape the 6'3"—a beauty of a board—and I was a Treehouse ambassador for a number of years.
2. 'Mexico missing students: Questions remain five years on', BBC News, 19 September 2019, www.bbc.com/news/world-latin-america-35539727.
3. Hernández, Anabel. *A Massacre in Mexico: The True Story Behind the Missing Forty-three Students,* trans. John Washington, Verso, New York, 2018.
4. McGahan, Jason. 'A bad break in Sinaloa: The true story of two surfers murdered in Mexico', *Men's Journal*, 6 May 2016, www.mensjournal.com/adventure/a-bad-break-in-sinaloa-two-surfers-murdered-in-mexico-w205312/.
5. 'Rancho Palo Alto'. International Surf Properties, www.internationalsurfproperties.com/listing/rancho-palo-alto.
6. Wall text for *Bordando otros males* by Miguel Hernández. 22 June – 13 October 2019, Museo Textil de Oaxaca.
7. Jiménez, Lluvia Sepúlveda. 'Comentarios a las obras' in *América. Visiones nuevas desde el viejo mundo*, publisher unnamed, 2019.
8. Lacey, Marc. 'Mexican man admits using acid on bodies—army says', *The New York Times*, 24 January 2009, www.nytimes.com/2009/01/25/world/americas/25mexico.html.
9. Trustytraveler82. 'What to say but read the review', Playa Carrizalillo, TripAdvisor, 21 June 2019, www.tripadvisor.com.au/Attraction_Review-g153373-d152482-Reviews-

Playa_Carrizalillo-Puerto_Escondido_Southern_Mexico. html#REVIEWS.

10. Nz_smarte. 'Crowded and local surfers own it', Playa Carrizalillo, TripAdvisor, 15 July 2018, www.tripadvisor. com.au/Attraction_Review-g153373-d152482-Reviews-or5-Playa_Carrizalillo-Puerto_Escondido_Southern_Mexico. html#REVIEWS.

11. Smith, Heidi. 'Unzipping Zipolite: tourist–local relationship in a backpacker enclave in Southern Mexico', thesis submission, University of Oslo, 2006, pdfs.semanticscholar. org/3a6d/173ff42a6c510063ead7525fef7536a02d41.pdf.

12. Villalobos, Juan Pablo. *Fiesta en la madriguera,* Editorial Anagrama, SA, Barcelona, 2010.

13. Villalobos, Juan Pablo and Harvey, Rosalind. 'Juan Pablo Villalobos', *Granta*, 12 January 2012, granta.com/interview-juan-pablo-villalobos.

14. Villalobos, Juan Pablo. '*Guardian* First Book award shortlist: Juan Pablo Villalobos', *The Guardian*, 12 November 2011, www.theguardian.com/books/2011/nov/11/guardian-first-book-juan-pablo-villalobos.

15. Villalobos, Juan Pablo. *Fiesta en la madriguera*, Editorial Anagrama, SA, Barcelona, 2010.

16. The translation 'braid of words' comes from Halfon, Eduardo. *The Polish Boxer*, trans. Daniel Hahn et al., Bellevue Literary Press, New York, 2012.

17. Taylor, Kimball. 'Indication Point', *Surfer*, 1 June 2015, www. surfer.com/features/indication-point.

18. de Ávila, Alejandro. *The Thorn and the Fruit: Plants from the Ethnobotanical Garden of Oaxaca*, Artes de México, Mexico City, 2006.

The Sea-affected Life—Mark Smith

1. Nettle, Stu. 'The reef revisited—interview with Mick Sowry', swellnet, 21 December 2015, www.swellnet.com/news/surfpolitik/2015/12/21/reef-revisited-interview-mick-sowry.

2. Morris, Linda. 'Interview: Favel Parrett', *Sydney Morning Herald*, 28 May 2011, www.smh.com.au/entertainment/books/interview-favel-parrett-20110526-1f5jn.html.

Other references:

Baker, Tim. *The Rip Curl Story*, Penguin Random House, Australia, 2019.

'Before Loutitt Bay', Lorne Historical Society, www.lornehistoricalsociety.org.au/history/before-loutitt-bay.

Boulton, Martin. 'Lunch with Henry Maas', *Sydney Morning Herald*, 12 September 2017, www.smh.com.au/entertainment/music/lunch-with-henry-maas-20170909-gye520.html.

'History & Profile', Wathaurong Aboriginal Co-operative, www.wathaurong.org.au/history-profile.

Manifold, Philomena. *Written in Stone: Reading the Rocks of the Great Ocean Road*, self-published, 2017.

Serong, Jock, ed. *Great Ocean Quarterly: Art, Ideas and the Sea*, vol. 1, no. 3.

Walker, Donald. *Beacons of Hope: An Early History of Cape Otway and King Island Lighthouses*, Neptune Press, Belmont, Victoria, 1981.

Don't You Know You've Got Legs?—Sally Breen

1. Byrne, J. and Houston, D. 'All that glitters: An environmental history "sketch" of Gold Coast City' in *Off the Plan: The Urbanisation of the Gold Coast*, ed. Caryl Bosman, Ayşin Dedekorkut-Howes, Andrew Leach, CSIRO Publishing, Victoria, 2016, p. 29.

2. Lyric from 'What I Got', Bradley Nowell, *Sublime*, 2006.

3. Molloy, Shannon. 'Australian surfing legend Mark "Occy" Occhilupo talks depression, substance abuse and getting sober', *news.com.au*, 7 November 2019, www.news.com.au/sport/sports-life/australian-surfing-legend-mark-occy-occhilupo-talks-depression-substance-abuse-and-getting-sober/news-story/575515877609671a99fba873367eaf2a.

4. Byrne and Houston, pp. 28–29.

5. As above, p. 19.
6. McPhee, D. 'Marine environments of the Gold Coast: Out with the old, in with the new', in *The Gold Coast Transformed: From Wilderness to Urban Ecosystem*, eds Tor Hundloe, Bridgette McDougall and Craig Page, CSIRO Publishing, Victoria, 2016, p. 86.
7. Lazzarow, N. and Tomlinson, R. 'Using observed market expenditure to estimate the value of recreational surfing to the Gold Coast, Australia', *Journal of Coastal Research*, Griffith Centre for Coastal Management, Queensland, 2009.
8. Pezman, Steve. 'The Evolutionary Surfer', *Surfer*, American Media, 1978.
9. Holiday, Ryan. *Ego Is the Enemy*, Portfolio (Penguin Classics), United States, 2016, p. 139.

The author is grateful for permission to reproduce from Caryl Bosman, Ayşin Dedekorkut-Howes and Andrew Leach (editors of compilation), *Off the Plan: The Urbanisation of the Gold Coast*, CSIRO Publishing, Victoria, 2016.

The Sea: Friend or Foe—Emily Brugman

1. Winton, Tim. *Land's Edge: A Coastal Memoir*, Pan Macmillan, Sydney, 1993, p. 84.
2. Arakwal Bumberlin People. 'Nguthungulli, Julian Rocks', *Arakwal People of Byron Bay: Significant Sites*, arakwal.com. au/nguthungulli.
3. Arakwal Bumberlin People. 'Three Sisters Rock', *Arakwal People of Byron Bay: Significant Sites*, arakwal.com.au/three-sisters-rock.
4. Beaulieu, Marie-Claire. *The Sea in the Greek Imagination*, University of Pennsylvania Press, Philadelphia, 2015, p. 3.
5. Winton, Tim. *Shallows,* Allen & Unwin, Sydney, 1984, p. 1.
6. Ashcroft, Bill. 'Water', *Tim Winton: Critical Essays*, eds Lyn McCredden and Nathanael O'Reilly, University of Western Australia Publishing, Crawley, WA, 2014, pp. 16–48: 32.

7. Adams, Michael. 'Salt blood', *Australian Book Review*, no. 392, 2017, p. 6, www.australianbookreview.com.au/abr-online/archive/2017/208-june-july-2017-no-392/4100-2017-calibre-essay-prize-winner-salt-blood.
8. As above.
9. Winton. *Shallows*, p. 109.
10. Ashcroft, p. 26.
11. As above, p. 28.
12. Freud, Sigmund. *Civilization and Its Discontents*, trans. Joan Riviere, ed. James Strachey, Hogarth Press and the Institute of Psycho-analysis, London, 1973, p. 8.
13. Irigaray, Luce. *An Ethics of Sexual Difference*, trans. Carolyn Burke and Gillian C. Gill, Cornell University Press, New York, 1993, p. 148.
14. Ashcroft, p. 41.
15. Melville, Herman. *Moby Dick* (first published in 1851), William Collins, Great Britain, 2013, p. 580.
16. As above, p. 572.
17. As above, p. 587.
18. As above, p. 588.
19. Beaulieu, p. 196.
20. As above, p. 197.
21. Homer. *The Odyssey*, Enriched Classics Edition, Simon & Schuster, New York, 2005, Book IV, p. 355.
22. Winton, Tim. *Breath*, Hamish Hamilton, Australia, 2008, p. 76.
23. Ashcroft, p. 35.
24. Adams, p. 6.
25. As above, p. 15.
26. Beaulieu, p. 10.
27. Ashcroft, p. 38.
28. Winton. *Shallows*, p. 74.

A Man Above the Reef—Jake Sandtner

1. Ronnie Blakey, Round One, Heat Ten: Fiji Pro 2016 WSL broadcast, www.worldsurfleague.com/posts/209172/2016-fiji-pro-round1-heat10-video.
2. Jake Sandtner, interview with Taj Burrow, Taj Burrow's hotel balcony, Burleigh Heads, Gold Coast, 15 May 2018.
3. Taj Burrow, 'Taj Burrow's teary goodbye', post–Fiji Pro 2016 WSL interview, www.worldsurfleague.com/posts/209400/taj-burrows-teary.
4. Martin Potter, 'The heavyweight bout featuring John John Florence and Taj Burrow lived up to the hype', post–Fiji Pro 2016 WSL interview, www.worldsurfleague.com/posts/210808/2016-fiji-pro-round-three-heat-10-video.
5. Taj Burrow, post–Fiji Pro 2016 WSL interview.
6. As above.
7. As above.
8. As above.
9. As above.
10. As above.
11. Will Swanton, 'Taj farewells the endless summer', 16 June 2016, The Australian, www.theaustralian.com.au/sport/taj-burrow-captured-my-eye-in-a-year-on-the-tour/news-story/17b3f46ae5d69e4bced2ce503c995dbc.

Acknowledgements

Sally Breen

Many people contributed to the formation of this piece. Thanks firstly to Jake Sandtner, my fellow contributor, for the introduction to the project and to Fremantle Press for having me—the editorial process has been an absolute pleasure thanks to the insights and keen reading eye of Georgia Richter. Thanks, too, to the crosshatch of surfers and friends who shared their stories: Tim Baker for his whale-sized insider knowledge, Zita for her unflinching honesty and Cheyne, Zara, Mike, Nick, Troy and a host of others for being open and being you. Thanks to Daryl Barnett, Chairman of Surf World Gold Coast, and to the city I call home for being so magnificently and unapologetically what it is.

Emily Brugman

A heartfelt thank you to Anne, Christine, Clare and Jill for allowing me to take part in your treasured morning ritual, for guiding me through the landscape below the waterline, for speaking so openly about your friendship with each other as well as with the ocean. Thank you to Tony Mowbray and his family, for welcoming me into your home, onto your boat, and sharing your rollicking seafaring story with me. Thank you to Mick Campbell and Tahlija Redgard, for your warmth and generosity, and your willingness to talk candidly about life and death and everything in between.

Sam Carmody

I feel indebted to many people for helping me come back from the period of time described in 'Hold-down'. During the worst of it all, I was bolstered by the company of visiting writers in the Northern Territory town of Batchelor, their talent and generosity and friendship. Special thank you to Samuel Wagan Watson for his gallows humour and writerly company. Thank you also to Adam Sharah for his sharp wit and compassion, and for the offer of those walks in the heat to the general store. Thank you to 'colleague' Courtney Collins, for the gentle wisdom offered over sweating drinks at the Rum Jungle Tavern after the day's classes. Thank you also to my smart and brilliant friend Kate Rendell. And Nicholas Jose. Your belief in my work kept me returning to the desk. To David Whish-Wilson for the gift of his mentorship, and the offer of that beer in Fremantle when things were at their darkest. Thank you to Georgia Richter for her guidance, the light at the surface she provided when I most struggled with this material. And finally to Mum and Dad. It is strengthening just knowing you are somewhere in the world. This is for you.

Madelaine Dickie

This story was written with the support of a Copyright Agency Ignite Grant and funding from the WA Department of Local Government, Sport and Cultural Industries. I would like to thank my dear friend Sabine Kirchleitner (Bina), for fielding constant questions during drafting and for that epic session at The Ranch. Zoë Barnard, thank you for your ever-sharp reflections on my work. This story is for my mum, Maggie, and my sister, Charlotte—I can't wait to see where our next wild family holiday will take us! It's also for Tom. My love, thank you for your addiction to adrenaline, and unwavering commitment to the pursuit of top-shelf fish and perfect surf.

Jake Sandtner

Firstly, I'd like to thank Taj Burrow for allowing me to pen this tale and share it with all of you. While this piece is my interpretation of our Honest Ale–fuelled interview, I extend Taj all my respect and thanks, for without him this book wouldn't exist. I'd also like to extend a huge thank you to Nigel Krauth, no longer just a mentor but a friend. I am beyond grateful for all his feedback, advice and assistance nuancing this piece. What a ride! The following people also deserve my thanks: Bow Edwards, for setting up interviews and meetings behind the scenes; Dr Sally Breen, for her assistance with early drafts; David Keay, for believing I could do it and allowing me time to do so; Griffith University, for giving me a go; and to my editor, Georgia Richter, who helped this piece reach its potential. Finally, I'd like to thank my fiancée, Eleanor, for her enduring support.

Mark Smith

I would like to thank Mick Sowry, Favel Parrett and Jeff Raglus for their generosity and commitment to seeing this story written. They gave freely of their time, their experiences, their memories and their unique artistic talents. It was a privilege to briefly engage in their worlds and I hope I have done them justice.

Contributors

Sally Breen lives on Queensland's Gold Coast. Her work has appeared widely in national and international journals and anthologies such as *Asia Literary Review, Meanjin, Open Road Review, The Age, The Best Australian Stories, Review of Australian Fiction, The Guardian UK, Verandah, Overland, The Australian, Hemingway Shorts* and *Griffith Review*. She is a regular contributor to *The Conversation*. Sally is the author of *The Casuals* (2011) and *Atomic City* (2013), which was shortlisted for the Queensland Literary Awards People's Choice Book of the Year in 2014. Sally is a senior lecturer in Writing and Publishing at Griffith University and a *Griffith Review* 2019 Queensland Writing Fellow.

Emily Brugman grew up surfing at Broulee, on the south coast of New South Wales. She currently lives in Mullumbimby, and works at Byron Writers Festival. She is a regular contributor to *Tracks* magazine, and her creative writing has appeared in *Overland, Verity La, Tincture Journal,* and the *UTS Writers' Anthology*. She is currently working on her first novel.

Sam Carmody is a novelist and WAM Award winning songwriter from Western Australia. His first novel, *The Windy Season*, won the 2017 Readings Prize for New Australian Fiction, and in 2018 he released his debut EP, *Shadow in the Dream*. He is currently based in Albany, Western Australia.

Madelaine Dickie's first novel, *Troppo*, won the City of Fremantle Hungerford Award in 2016 and was shortlisted for the Dobbie Literary Award and the Barbara Jefferis Award. Her second novel, *Red Can Origami*, was written on Balangarra country in the Kimberley region of Western Australia, and at Youkobo Art Space in Tokyo, Japan. A surf obsession has led Madelaine from Spain's Mundaka, to Namibia's Skeleton Coast, to little-known waves in the Dominican Republic. In 2019, she spent three and a half months writing and surfing in Mexico. She is studying Spanish and speaks Indonesian. Madelaine currently lives in Exmouth, Western Australia.

Jake Sandtner is currently completing a PhD at Griffith University on the Gold Coast. Jake spends his day job in marketing and design. When not writing, you can find Jake cruising coastlines, enjoying a cold beer or disrupting his cat's sleeping habits. He is a sucker for motorbikes, a half-hearted photographer, surf lover and a devoted bookworm.

Mark Smith lives on Victoria's west coast. A surfer for the past forty-five years, his boards have got longer and thicker in direct correlation to his shoulders getting older and stiffer. His debut novel, *The Road to Winter* (2016), was shortlisted for multiple awards and is taught in schools around Australia. The sequel, *Wilder Country* (2017), won the 2018 Australian Indie Book Award for YA. The third book in the trilogy, *Land of Fences*, was published in 2019. Mark is also an award-winning writer of short fiction, with credits including the Josephine Ulrick Literature Prize and the Alan Marshall Short Story Prize, and his work has appeared in *Best Australian Stories*, *Review of Australian Fiction*, *The Big Issue*, *The Victorian Writer* and *The Australian*. He'd trade them all for two new shoulders.

First published 2021 by FREMANTLE PRESS.
Fremantle Press Inc. trading as Fremantle Press
25 Quarry Street, Fremantle WA 6160
(PO Box 158, North Fremantle WA 6159)
www.fremantlepress.com.au

Cover design by Nada Backovic, www.nadabackovic.com.
Cover images: Beach, Lachlan Dempsey; Surfboard, Nicolas Pereyra, both
   unsplash.com.
Printed by McPherson's Printing, Victoria, Australia.

 A catalogue record for this
book is available from the
National Library of Australia

ISBN 9781760990329 (paperback)
ISBN 9781760990336 (ebook)

Fremantle Press is supported by the State Government through
the Department of Local Government, Sport and Cultural Industries.

Publication of this title was assisted by the Commonwealth Government
through the Australia Council, its arts funding and advisory body.